SpringerBriefs in Ethics

For further volumes:
http://www.springer.com/series/10184

Andreas Krieg

Motivations for Humanitarian Intervention

Theoretical and Empirical Considerations

Springer

Andreas Krieg
War and Defence Studies
King's College London
London
UK

ISSN 2211-8101 ISSN 2211-811X (electronic)
ISBN 978-94-007-5373-0 ISBN 978-94-007-5374-7 (eBook)
DOI 10.1007/978-94-007-5374-7
Springer Dordrecht Heidelberg New York London

Library of Congress Control Number: 2012944386

Printed on acid-free paper

Springer is part of Springer Science+Business Media (www.springer.com)

Contents

Part II The Empirical Analysis

Abbreviations

AGOA	The African Growth Opportunity Act
CARE	Cooperative for Assistance and Relief Everywhere
CNN	Cable News Network
DPKO	The United Nations Department of Peacekeeping Operations
EC	The European Community
ECOWAS	The Economic Community of West African States
EU	The European Union
HLPR	The High Level Panel on Threats, Challenges and Change
IAEA	The International Atomic Energy Agency
ICC	The International Criminal Court
ICISS	The International Commission on Intervention and State Sovereignty
ICRC	The International Committee of the Red Cross
INTERFET	The International Force For East Timor
KLA	The Kosovo Liberation Army
NATO	The North Atlantic Treaty Organization
NSS	National Security Strategy
RPF	Rwandan People's Front
RUF	Revolutionary United Front
SLA	The Sudanese Liberation Army
TF1	Télévision Française 1
UN	The United Nations
UNAMIR	The United Nations Assistance Mission for Rwanda
UNAMSIL	The United Nations Assistance Mission in Sierra Leone
UNSC	The United Nations Security Council
UNHCR	The United Nations High Commissioner for Refugees
US	The United States of America
WMD	Weapons of Mass Destruction

Introduction

»Massacre, rape, ethnic cleansing, state terrorism, contemporary versions of "bastard feudalism," complete with ruthless warlords and lawless bands of armed men: these are the acts and occasions that invite us, or require us, to override the presumption against moving armies across borders and using force inside countries that have not threatened or attacked their neighbours. There is no external aggression to worry about, only domestic brutality, civil war, political tyranny, ethnic or religious persecution«[1]

The fall of the Iron Curtain and the subsequent disintegration of the Eastern Bloc in the beginning of the 1990s mark one of the major turning points in contemporary history. It brought about major changes in the international arena and the power relations between its major players. New conflicts arose or old conflicts reappeared that were previously suppressed by the static nature of the Cold War system. In addition, globalization whose roots can be found in the 1980s, accelerated a development of regional and ethnic upheaval, particularly in the periphery of the international system. In face of rising internal conflicts devastating entire regions and populations, the United Nations and the then leading super power, the United States, were seeking new approaches to address these conflicts. The rather state-centric and sovereignty-based international system underwent a regime change allowing for the occurrence of a new phenomenon in international law: military humanitarian intervention. Military humanitarian intervention, i.e. any coercive action, up to and including the use of force, with the alleged purpose of preventing or putting to halt gross and massive violations of human rights, was a result of a new mindset that occurred in international relations in the early 1990s.

Although though humanitarian intervention became a practised custom already in the early 1990s, the concept itself remains poorly defined in international law, which remains dominated by notions of unrestrained state sovereignty and the

---

[1] Walzer, M. (1995). The Politics of Rescue. *Social Research*. Volume: 62. Issue: 1, pp. 51ff. New York: The New School of Social Research. (p. 53)

non-intervention principle. While international lawyers did not make the effort to redefine the concept of intervention, just war theorists began to approach the phenomenon from various angles. Humanitarian intervention as a concept ultimately employing the use of force was and still is assessed against the background of just war theory and the question of what constitutes a righteous and just intervention. The two most prominent normative theories, offering approaches to the intervention for humanitarian purposes, can be identified as liberal cosmopolitanism and realism. While cosmopolitanists regard individuals and their rights as the essence of international relations, realists believe that the state and its rights are the most important values to be protected. It follows that cosmopolitanists perceive interventions with the sole or primary purpose of saving or protecting suffering individuals as righteous. Realists, on the contrary, pursue an approach of minimal solidarism, namely denouncing any intervention as unrighteous that has not the primary purpose of protecting the interests of the nation or the state. Hence, at the core of the debate in just war theory lays the question of whether states should intervene to protect the interests of states or the interests of individuals. Related to this problem is the question of whether humanitarian interventions are supposed to be motivated by altruistic or national interest-related considerations. While realists claim humanitarian interventions in the past were driven by national or self-interests, cosmopolitanists might recognize degrees of altruistic motivation factors.

In this book I will focus on the motivation for humanitarian intervention and I intend to shed light on the question of what motivates Western democracies to intervene or abstain from intervention when confronted with a humanitarian crisis. This study attempts to provide an answer to the question of what different factors motivated humanitarian intervention in the past and to what extent these factors express the degree of altruism or national/self-interest involved in the decision to intervene. Is it cosmopolitanism or realism that brings about the most appropriate assessment of the motivation of military humanitarian interventions in the last two decades?

Answering this question is both relevant for the debate in academia as well as for policy making. This research question will be answered against the backdrop of the century old normative debate about what constitutes a just war. Analyzing all the cases of past humanitarian interventions as well as several non-intervention cases, the results of this research contribute to the debate about the importance of national interests in foreign policy as well as the extent to which altruism may be considered a variable in foreign policy decision making. Moreover, the results of this research grant policy makers insights into the actual motivation behind the humanitarian interventions of the past. As we enter into the second decade of the twenty-first century, one may not rule out the possibility that civilian populations worldwide will be increasingly threatened by sub-or supranational forces in the absence of national protection. Consequently, the international community will be ever more morally obliged to manage humanitarian catastrophes. Hence, knowing what triggers intervention and non intervention will help to make the necessary policy changes to ensure coherent and credible responses to humanitarian crises in the future.

The empirical analysis conducted in this book will rely upon both a qualitative and quantitative approach. The motivation for intervention in all cases of humanitarian intervention since 1990 will be qualitatively analyzed. Then, based on the parameters put forth to measure the extent to which intervention decisions were motivated by altruistic and national/self-interest factors, the qualitative analysis is translated into quantitative values. This quantitative dimension allows to give a holistic picture of all intervention and non-intervention cases whereas also allowing for a cross-case analysis demonstrating the relative value of the motivation in various humanitarian intervention cases.

This book will be divided into two essential parts, a normative and an empirical part, which though related do provide different contributions to the question of what motivates military humanitarian intervention. While the first part of the book will develop a normative argument mostly based on cosmopolitanism and realism about what ought to motivate humanitarian intervention, the second part will present an empirical analysis of what actually motivated humanitarian intervention. I commence the normative part of the book by giving an introduction to the legal and moral legitimacy of humanitarian intervention. In order to understand the academic debate in just war theory, one has to comprehend the evolution of the concept of humanitarian intervention both in international law and political theories. Further, I continue to analyze the position of national interests and altruism in international relations and present arguments for and against the prevalence of these factors in international relations. Following the normative part I will present the empirical results of the qualitative analysis of the various cases after giving a comprehensive overview over the research method employed in this book and presenting the six-parameter measure. The qualitative data presented will then be translated into quantitative values that are statistically analyzed and evaluated. I conclude this book with a discussion of the research question and the implications of the findings for both academia and real life policy making.

Part I
The Normative Debate

Chapter 1
The Legal and Moral Legitimacy of Intervention

This chapter gives a comprehensive introduction to the background against which the concept of humanitarian intervention has to be understood. Outlining the evolution of the international state system from a purely state centric to a poly-centric system, this chapter touches upon the impact of the turn of the era in 1990 on various realms of international relations, political ethics and international law. The occurrence of military intervention for humanitarian purposes has marked the introduction into a new era, where traditional concepts of sovereignty and the nation state were gradually replaced by more cosmopolitan notions. After clarifying the new international legal environment, this chapter will present the various positions in just war theory for the moral legitimacy of intervention.

1.1 The Impact of Globalization on the International State System

The evolution of the state system towards the end of the 20th century had a crucial impact on the emergence of the concept of humanitarian intervention. The break-up of the Eastern Bloc and the shift from a bipolar to a unipolar world were arguably the most important factors in creating a new world order. While the major powers were moving away from an era of confrontation towards an era of cooperation and collaboration, the foreign policy agenda of the West became occupied with the aftermath of the disengagement of the East—West alignment. The sharp increase of intra-state conflicts, trans-state conflicts and civil wars in the 1990s was believed by many to be directly linked to the dissolution of the Cold War World Order.[1] As a consequence of these developments the major powers were not preparing anymore for an armed attack by the ideological opponent but were engaging in small scale conflicts far away from their own territory helping to make

---

[1] Bose and Perotti (2002).

A. Krieg, *Motivations for Humanitarian Intervention*, SpringerBriefs in Ethics, DOI: 10.1007/978-94-007-5374-7_1, © The Author(s) 2013

the world a safer place through the promotion of democracy and social justice as well as the alleviation of poverty.[2]

Although one could argue that the collapse of the Cold War political system has facilitated or even contributed to the rise of a New World Order one must not disregard one of the major developments that already set in prior to the relaxation of the East–West relations: globalization. Despite the fact that the historical origins of globalization are still subject to an ongoing debate, one can assert that the geopolitical as well as social developments underlying the process of globalization set in years before the first signs of the end of the Cold War became apparent.

Giddens (1990) defines globalization as "[…] the intensification of worldwide social relations which link distant localities in such a way that local happenings are shaped by events occurring many miles away and vice versa […]".[3] Another definition focusing more on the interconnectedness between localities describes globalization as a "[…] process of increasing interconnectedness between societies such that events in one part of the world more and more have effects on people and societies far away[…]".[4] While these definitions focus on the most important factors of the phenomenon, they nonetheless lack the holistic nature of Rosenau's definition of globalization. Rosenau (1999) characterizes globalization as

> […] the microelectronic revolution that has facilitated the rapid flow of ideas, information, pictures, and money across continents; the transportation revolution that has hastened the boundary-spanning flow of elites, tourists, immigrants (legal and illegal), migrants, and whole populations; the organizational revolution that has shifted the flow of authority, influence and power beyond traditional boundaries, and the economic revolution that has redirected the flow of goods, services, capital, and ownership among countries. Taken together, these flows have resulted in the globalization of local, provincial, national and international affairs—a cumulative process that is both the source and consequence of eroding boundaries, integrating regions, proliferating networks, diminishing territorial attachments, coalescing social movements, weakening states, contracting sovereignty, dispersing authority, demanding publics, and expanding citizen skills-all of which serve as underpinnings of the age of fragmentation […].[5]

Going hand in hand with the debate about the erosion of the nation state's territoriality is the debate about the concept of sovereignty in the era of globalization; a debate that becomes essential in understanding the impact of globalization on the international state system today. Together with the global social and economic interconnectivity arising towards the end of the 20th century, also politics experienced a shift from state centric towards geocentric global politics. State sovereignty and autonomy have been compromised by international regimes that increasingly shape the policy making of nation states and thereby impact the lives of individuals homogenously across national borders.

---

[2] Ibid (p. 263).

[3] Giddens (1990).

[4] Smith et al. (2001).

[5] Rosenau (1999).

In the 17th century's Westphalian interpretation of the term, sovereignty referred to the two core principles: (1) *rex est imperator in regno suo* and (2) *cuius regio, eius religio.* While the former principle points to the internal sovereignty of a state, namely the fact that there is only one central authority in the state, the latter is concerned with the external sovereignty of the state, notably its right of independence and non-interference from an external party.[6] State sovereignty is often defined in terms of internal control and external autonomy; however, this definition does not hold in the real world of politics where control and autonomy become a blurry concept. Therefore, it might be more sensible to define sovereignty as authority to "[...] rule over a delimited territory and the population residing in it [...]".[7] Apart from the internal attribute of state sovereignty, sovereignty expresses itself substantially in the recognition of a particular state by the community of peers (states).[8] The erosion of known concepts of territoriality, identity and social affiliation have created feelings of socio-political disintegration, which raised a call for the establishment of universal norms that could bring order to the arising chaos. The problems of the globalized world are global issues of economic, social and ecological nature. In particular policy areas such as counter-terrorism, human rights, pollution and crime receive high transnational attention.[9] In order to deal with these issues effectively, international collaboration beyond national borders and national sovereignty became necessary. In the era of globalization political power and political activity has extended beyond national borders and has created a complex network of official and unofficial actors that compete with the sovereign nation state for policy agenda shaping. Gradually the sovereign nation state had to sacrifice some of its absolute sovereign features on the altar of global cooperation in order to be able to survive the pressure arising from transnational threats.[10] The nation state of the Westphalian world order with its full and uncompromised sovereignty and autonomy ceased to exist. Therefore, scholars define the globalized world order already as post-Westphalian. The idea of territoriality has changed since borders only remain important for administration purposes. A new geography of political organization and political power is emerging which transcends territories and borders. The concept of state sovereignty only persists in an altered manner because authority and sovereign power of national governments have been transformed in a competitive environment between national, regional and global entities. Further, the aspect of state autonomy, also essential for the nation state of the Westphalian world order, is compromised as national governments are forced to engage in multilateral collaboration and cooperation. Thus, one can state that simultaneously with the increasing mobility of information, goods and people, the conservative notion of

6 Helmke (2004).

7 Ayoob (2002).

8 Ibid.

9 Held et al. (1999).

10 Ibid (p.50).

the nation state has been diminished in face of a global governance complex embracing states, international institutions, and transnational networks, i.e. agencies which function to promote, regulate or intervene in the common affairs of humanity.[11]

Despite the ongoing globalization of politics and economics, the nation state as such has not ceased to exist. The nation state is arguably still the most important organizing tool in the international arena; however its role in international relations has changed through the rising importance of local, regional and supranational actors in the international arena.[12] Thus, even though the nation state in its Westphalian nature with its unlimited sovereignty does not exist anymore, the nation state nonetheless remains the most important actor among few, which has not yet lost its exclusive role as a legitimate decision maker in international relations.

Another important aspect shaped by globalization is the nature of conflict itself. As it has been established above, globalization describes a phenomenon of social, economic and political upheaval on a global scale beyond national borders. In particular the increasing permeability of state borders and the continuing circumcision of nation state sovereignty have had a deep impact on the way conflicts arise and how these conflicts are fought. Most of the post-1990 interventions by the major players of world politics have been in conflicts that can be described as globalized or new conflicts, namely conflicts that in their character can be clearly differentiated from conventional conflicts. Kaldor (1999) describes these new conflicts as 'globalized' since they are characterized by a highly fragmentized and decentralized state, private military actors that do not operate within the conservative framework of state sovereignty and military forces that are in no respect accountable to any centralized political power.[13] Weiss (2007) defines four essential characteristics that distinguish globalized conflicts from past conflicts:

> [...] First, the locus of war no longer coincides with state borders—in areas of fragmented authority, in fact, borders are often meaningless. Second instead of states and their militaries being main agents, non-state actors are playing an increasing role. Third, the economies of war are no longer financed principally from government tax revenues but increasingly from illicit activities, aid, and plunder. Fourth, instead of combatants being the main victims, civilians are increasingly paying the lion's share of costs [...].[14]

These characteristics can be found in almost all conflicts after 1990 that have created the setting for humanitarian crises in the last two decades.

Hence, reducing the geopolitical and social upheavals after 1990 back to the disintegration of the Eastern Bloc would only tell one side of a story, which began already decades before Gorbachev spoke about *Perestroika* and *Glasnost.*[15]

---

11 McGrew (2001).

12 Held et al. Op cit. 10 (p. 441).

13 Kaldor (1999).

14 Weiss (2007).

15 Kishlansky (2001).

The actual socio-economic and political upheaval that changed global politics in way that concepts of sovereignty, autonomy and territoriality had to be redefined was globalization, which became apparent in the political realm only in the 1990s. Thus, both a combination of the transformation of power relations and the break-up of conventional concepts of society and statehood through globalization set the beginning of a new era where norms of non-intervention and state sovereignty have to be redefined in order to allow intervention for humanitarian purposes.

1.2 Intervention in International Law Since 1945

1.2.1 Definition of Intervention

Humanitarian Intervention, namely the "[…] coercive action by states involving the use of armed force in another state […] for the purpose of preventing or putting to a halt gross and massive violations of human rights or international humanitarian law […]",[16] appeared as a concept in international relations only after military action on behalf of suffering individuals became a political custom in the early 1990s.[17] Whereas the term humanitarian intervention initially referred to an intervention by mostly Western states to save their own citizens from harm abroad, over time the definition of the concept was extended so as to include the protection of foreign nationals from inhumane treatment of their government. What do I imply when speaking about the concept of 'humanitarian intervention'?

The combination of the words 'humanitarian' and 'intervention' constitutes an oxymoron that combines the concept of benevolence with a term that in international law is closely connected to the use of force.[18] The term 'intervention' on its own is described by scholars adhering to the classical notion as a dictatorial interference by one state into the affairs of another state. Interference itself can come in various forms ranging from political or economic coercion to the actual use of armed force.[19] In more detail intervention by itself can be defined as an "[…] activity undertaken by a state, a group within a state, a group of states or an international organization which interferes coercively in the domestic affairs of another state […]".[20] What is important to note here is the emphasis on the interference of one state into the domestic affairs of another state, thereby crossing a line in international law, as the sovereignty of the receiving state is violated. International politics in history have often been dominated by the aim to influence other states' policies through either diplomatic or economic pressure as well as the

---

16 Ryter (2003).

17 Domagala (2004).

18 Roberts (1993).

19 Oppenheim (1955).

20 Vincent (1974).

use of force. According to Finnemore (2003) one of the core objectives of intervention is to change 'political authority structure', an assignment that can be fulfilled by various means of interference with the domestic affairs of another state.[21] The term 'humanitarian' designates the primary purpose of intervention, namely averting or holding violations of fundamental human rights that 'shock the conscience of mankind'. The actual threshold for a legitimate intervention will be discussed later in this book.

Putting these two terms together humanitarian intervention can be defined as

> [...] coercive action by states involving the use of armed force in another state without the consent of its government, with or without the authorization from the United Nations Security Council, for the purpose of preventing or putting to a halt gross and massive violations of human rights or international humanitarian law [...].[22]

Another definition by Tom Farer (2005) states that the intervention for humanitarian purposes entails

> [...] the threat or use of force across state borders by a state (or group of states) aimed at preventing or ending widespread and grave violations of fundamental human rights of persons other than the nationals of the intervening state and without the permission of the state within which force is applied [...].[23]

This definition adds an essential aspect of humanitarian intervention: unlike conventional military operations, which are more likely directly concerned with defending the nation, the state or its citizens, humanitarian intervention is widely understood as an armed intervention for the purpose of saving lives of strangers. Thereby, military intervention receives a fairly altruistic or philanthropic dimension.[24] Consequently, humanitarian intervention is a military act that is conducted in order to relieve the suffering of individuals and therefore has to be carried out under guidelines of limited force so as not to deteriorate the suffering on the ground.

Even though humanitarian intervention in its contemporary form only came about in the 1990s, the roots of humanitarian intervention can be traced back to the philosophical debates of natural law in the 16th century where scholars such as the Spanish Suárez noted that the legitimacy of intervention should not be granted "[...] except in circumstances in which the slaughter of innocent people and similar wrongs take place [...]".[25] This idea was picked up by Johann Jakob Moser in the late 18th century who referred to the state's right to intervene to protect individuals from religious persecution.[26] With the turn of the 19th century

---

[21] Finnemore (2003)).

[22] Ryder (2003) Op. Cit. 17 (p.5).

[23] Farer et al. (2005).

[24] Finnemore Op. Cit. 22 (p.10).

[25] Knudsen (2009).

[26] Stowell (1921).

international lawyers predominantly envisaged a right to intervene on grounds of humanity, i.e.

> [...] should the cruelty be so long continued and so revolting that the best instincts of human nature are outraged by it, and should an opportunity arise for bringing it to an end [...] there is nothing in the law of nations which will brand as a wrongdoer the state that steps forward and undertakes the necessary intervention. [...].[27]

Due to increasing military and humanitarian activity under the direction of the UN in conflicts in the past two decades, the term humanitarian intervention is oftentimes used interchangeably with peacekeeping operations. Despite the humanitarian character of both types of engagement, peacekeeping differs from humanitarian intervention in that it is not a form of intervention, i.e. does not rely on any coercive action of states against another state and is usually not entitled to use force. Peacekeeping operations usually appear after the conflict has been officially settled through a peace agreement. The UN Department of Peacekeeping Operations (DPKO) illustrates the three core objectives of peacekeeping as follows: first of all, peacekeeping operations assist in maintenance of cease-fires, supervise the implementation of comprehensive settlements, or protect humanitarian operations. Thus, peacekeeping operations unlike humanitarian interventions are not coercive in character as they manage post-conflict situations that do not require participating troops to use means of coercion but rather require its troops to provide supervising and administrative assistance.[28]

In this book humanitarian intervention will be defined as any coercive action, up to and including the use of force, with the alleged purpose of preventing or putting to halt gross and massive violations of human rights, with or without the consent of the receiving state as well as with or without the authorization of the UN Security Council.

1.2.2 The Principles of Sovereignty and Non-Intervention in the UN System

Humanitarian Intervention as a foreign policy tool has only appeared recently and constitutes a dilemma in an international law system that has been barely reformed since the First World War. When the old Balance-of-Power system came to an end after the break-up of the Old Europe in Versailles in 1919, Western states envisaged a global state system that would support nation states in their strife for peace.[29] However, it was the devastating experience of the failure of the League of Nations system during World War II that prompted the international community to

[27] Lawrence (1925).

[28] UN Department for Peacekeeping Operations (2009) What is peacekeeping? Retrieved October 22nd, 2009 from http://www.un.org/Depts/dpko/dpko/field/body_pkeep.htm

[29] Shaw (1995).

establish an international regulatory body strong enough to keep the peace. In the Charter of the newly founded United Nations (UN) the signatories asserted the primary purpose of the UN to"[...] to save succeeding generations from the scourge of war, which twice in our lifetime has brought untold sorrow to mankind [...]".[30]The United Nations Charter was signed in 1945 to lay a foundation for an international law system that was based on the one hand on the century-old rejection of the use of force and on the other hand based on the sacrosanct notion of state sovereignty deriving from the Peace of Westphalia 1648.

The sovereignty of its Member States is central to the UN system, as all Member States are regarded as equals whose sovereignty is inviolable. Sovereignty is considered the most significant norm in international relations that functions as a shield against the ambitions of external intervention into the domestic affairs of a state. Therefore, the founders of the United Nations established the sovereignty principle as a major prerequisite for the upholding of peace and stability in the international arena.[31] That is to say, as a basic principle Member States as well as the organization itself do not recognize a higher authority than the state. It follows that the United Nations is designed as a purely intergovernmental organization, which does not accept any other source of superior jurisdiction than the individual nation state.[32] Consequently, the contemporary state system relying on the codified laws of the United Nations is *de jure* not different from the Westphalian state system evolving around the fixed and statist notion of territoriality, a clear concept of state sovereignty as a government's entitlement to supreme, unqualified, and exclusive political and legal authority, and finally a clear concept of autonomy based on the principle of self-determination.[33] As the integrity and sovereignty of the nation state lays at the very core of the United Nations, intervention and especially the use of force are concepts that in the post-1945 international system are considered illegal or only legitimate under exceptional circumstances.

As mentioned earlier on in this book, intervention constitutes a coercive interference by a state into the domestic affairs of another state, thereby violating the sovereignty and autonomy of the receiving state. Due to the fact that intervention itself is closely linked to the use of force, the UN Charter strongly objects intervention as it violates the sovereignty principle. Art. 2(4) UN states explicitly that "[...] all members shall refrain in their international relations from the threat or use of force against the territorial integrity or political independence of any state [...]".[34] Using force against the 'territorial integrity or political independence of any state' has been further explained in the 1965 Declaration on the Inadmissibility of Intervention in the Domestic Affairs of States by stating that

---

30 United Nations (1945).

31 Shaw Op. Cit. 30 (p. 41).

32 Taylor and Curtis (2007).

33 McGrew Op. Cit. 12 (p.23).

34 United Nations Op. Cit. 31 (Art. 2 (4)).

> [...] no state has the right to intervene, directly or indirectly, for any reason whatsoever, in the internal or external affairs of any other state. Consequently, armed intervention and all other forms of interference or attempted threats against the personality of the state or against its political, economic and cultural elements, are condemned [...].[35]

This exemplification of the prohibition of the use of force clearly states that intervention has to be understood as being equal to the use of force and is thereby condemned as illegal.

The principle of sovereignty and non-intervention even goes that far so as to also limit the UN's organizational authority to intervene in Member States' internal policies. Art. 2 (7) UN holds that "Nothing contained in the present Charter shall authorize the United Nations to intervene in matters which are essentially within the domestic jurisdiction of any state [...]".[36] This clause clearly presents the character of the UN system as an organization that sanctifies the sovereignty of its Member States and compromises its own decision making power and values with the inviolability of the integrity of its Member States.

The UN Charter permits the use of force only under one circumstance: as an act of self-defence where a state responds with the lawful force against an unlawful force.[37] Article 51 UN states that "[...] nothing in the present charter shall impair the inherent right of individual or collective self-defence if an armed attack occurs [...]".[38] However, any act to restore peace and stability must be referred to and authorized by the Security Council before the act of self-defence occurs. That is to say that 'lawful force' requires the authorization of the Security Council, as it is according to Art. 33/36/37 UN the primary institution of the UN to decide on the nature of an aggressive action and the appropriate response to it.[39] Any non-authorized intervention in civil wars, aiding authorities of a state, aiding rebels, facilitating self-determination and even humanitarian intervention have to be rejected as illegitimate actions in face of the sovereignty principle and codified international law.[40] Collective coercive action under the authorization of the UN Security Council in cases of threats to peace, breaches of peace, and overt aggression are the only cases that are deemed legitimate according to the narrow interpretation of international law.[41]

Conclusively one can state that in the international system of today which is legally still bound to a state system of the Westphalian era, the sovereignty of states is at least *de jure* sacred. Thus,

> If a state has a right to sovereignty, this implies that other states have a duty to respect that right by, among other things, refraining from intervention in its domestic affairs [...]

---

35 United Nations General Assembly (1965).

36 United Nations Op. Cit. 31(Art. 2 (7).

37 Bjorna (2009).

38 United Nations Op.Cit. 31 (Art. 51).

39 Bjorna Op. Cit. 38 (p. 49).

40 Shaw Op. Cit. 30 (p. 721ff.).

41 Smith (1998).

> The function of the principle of non-intervention in international relations might be said, then, to be one of protecting the principle of state sovereignty [...].[42]

Hence, for the sake of lasting peace and stability, the UN legal system has invested highly into demonizing intervention as an act of aggression, thereby granting sovereigns in their realm the privilege of indefeasibility.

However, as much as codified international law takes a restrictionist approach to the intervention of one state into the domestic affairs of another, counter-restrictionists are more lenient in their interpretation of the UN's legal framework. Counter-restrictionist argue that the UN legal system does provide sufficient legal base for intervention on humanitarian purposes since first the UN Charter commits states to protecting fundamental human rights and second humanitarian intervention has become a custom in international law. According to counter-restrictionists human rights have just as important a role in the UN Charter as peace and security.[43] Under Art. 1 (3) UN, the international community under the umbrella of the United Nations commits itself "[...] to achieve international cooperation in solving international problems of [...] humanitarian character, and in promoting and encouraging respect for human rights and for fundamental freedoms for all [...]".[44] Looking at this article it remains questionable how the community is to solve international problems of humanitarian character without harming the sovereignty of the respective state. Article 55 and 56 UN highlight the importance of human rights for the organization again without backing up the plea for the promotion of human rights with a credible legal instrument that has the ability to actually implement these provisions. Counter-restrictionist, however, continue their argument by stating that the provisions of Art. 1(3), 55 and 56 UN would be sufficient for the UN Security Council to circumvent Art. 2 (4) and legitimately authorize intervention in cases of massive human rights abuse, mass murder or genocide.[45]

Moreover, the Genocide Convention, another legal tool of the UN system that has been adopted by the General Assembly in 1948, addresses crimes of genocide more specifically and even foresees punishments for the violation of the Convention.[46] The Genocide Convention is the only legal imperative in international law authorizing the use of all necessary means including the use of force to halt domestic human rights abuses that constitute genocide.[47] Under Art. IV of the Convention it is laid down that "[...] Persons committing genocide or any of the other acts enumerated in article III shall be punished, whether they are constitutionally responsible rulers, public officials or private individuals [...]".[48] The binding nature of this Convention is further exemplified in the ICJ's Advisory

---

42 Vincent RJ Op. Cit.21 (p.14).

43 Wheeler and Bellamy (2008).

44 United Nations Op. Cit. 31 (Art. 1 (3).

45 Reisman (1985).

46 McQueen (2006).

47 Ibid

48 United Nations General Assembly (1948).

Opinion on Reservations to the Genocide Convention issued in 1951. The ICJ clearly states that even though the nature of the Convention and its provisions are considered to be fundamental principles of the UN system and were adopted by majority vote in the General Assembly, the Convention is not generally binding for all states. Only states that have signed and ratified the Convention are subject to the provisions laid down in the Convention.[49] Despite the fact that until today a quarter of the UN Member States did not sign or accede to the Genocide Convention, the most influential powers have done so. In addition to the lack of universal character of the Convention, the Genocide Convention is further limited in its application to the crime of genocide as it does not extend to other crimes under international law such as war crimes or crimes against humanity. Despite the fact that the convention explicitly condemns acts of genocide as a punishable act under international law, the convention lacks the necessary precision to actually specify how perpetrators are to be held accountable for their wrongdoing. Particularly, the convention does not address the question of how to trial a legitimate ruler of a sovereign country without violating the sovereignty.

Even counter-restrictionists who do not find the references to human rights in the UN Charter sufficiently strong to legitimize intervention, find it difficult to deny the argument that customary international law through state practise might provide a legal base permitting humanitarian intervention. When a representative number of states engages into a certain practise convinced that their actions are legally justifiable on basis of codified law or the practise has the status of law, states can create through a so-called *opinion juris* a custom that eventually receives an equal status to codified law as soon as other states join in on that practise or tolerate this practise as lawful.[50] In the counter-restrictionist belief, the custom of intervention for humanitarian purposes has preceded the UN legal system, evidenced by an allied intervention in Greece (1827) or American intervention in Cuba (1898). The post 1990 era has given the *opinion juris* even more credibility as humanitarian intervention appeared to have occurred as an accepted and common practise by a large number of major powers.[51] Nonetheless, one must not overrate the consensus in the international community of the right to intervene in the domestic affairs of another state. Whereas a wide range of Western states supports intervention to halt or avert acute humanitarian crisis, other major powers such as China or Russia hold on to the sovereignty principle in its purest form.

1.2.3 Intervention in International Law Since 1990

The era following the break-up of the Eastern Bloc has witnessed a sharp increase of interventions that have been justified partially or entirely by humanitarian

---

49 The International Court of Justice (1951).

50 Shaw Op. Cit. 30 (p. 74.).

51 Wheeler and Bellamy (2008) Op.Cit. 44 (p. 526).

considerations. This new era was introduced by President Bush in a speech in 1990 as a New World Order that will create a world

> [...] *freer from the threat of terror, stronger in the pursuit of justice, and more secure in the quest for peace. An era in which the nations of the world, East and West, North and South, can prosper and live in harmony* [...] *A world in which nations recognize the shared responsibility for freedom and justice. A world where the strong respect the rights of the weak.* [...].[52]

The first step into the new era was Operation Desert Storm, where a broad coalition freed Kuwait from Iraqi occupation with the authorization of the UN Security Council. The First Gulf War marks a turning point in the foreign policy outlook of the major powers after the Second World War. Instead of fighting a war to contain the spread of the ideological opponent's influence, the First Gulf War was a collective act of self-defence under Chapter VII of the UN Charter assisting Kuwait in freeing itself from Iraqi oppression similar to the Korean War. The actual defining moment of Operation Desert Storm lies in the aftermath of the collective intervention of the West in Kuwait, bringing about the first humanitarian intervention to save the endangered population in Northern Iraq.

Following the victory of the coalition forces in 1991 a humanitarian crisis in Iraq's Northern part of Kurdistan led to the intervention of the US and allies to bring the human suffering to an end. UN Security Council Resolution 688 (1991) authorizing the intervention, for the first time linked human suffering to a threat to international peace and security.[53] The UN SC Resolution 688 (1991) marks the entrance of the UN system and of the international community into a new era that was not merely dominated anymore by maintaining international peace and security, but also by a more active commitment to maintaining fundamental human rights around the globe. The suffering of the civilian population on the ground caused by Iraq's government's repression is condemned by the Security Council in the Resolution. The Security Council "[...] condemns the repression of the Iraqi civilian population in many parts of Iraq, including most recently in Kurdish-populated areas, the consequences of which threaten international peace and security in the region [...]".[54] Thus, in order to justify the multilateral intervention on basis of international law deriving from the UN Charter, the Security Council used the reference to regional peace and security. Despite the fact that the UN SC Res. 688 (1991) does not refer back to any human rights provisions, the resolution constitutes a formal justification by a UN organ of an intervention into a sovereign state for humanitarian concerns.

The next decisive step into a new era was the appointment of Boutros Boutros Ghali as UN Secretary General in 1992 who was determined to allow for the UN system to become more flexible in terms of intervention for humanitarian purposes and individual human justice. Witnessing the consequences of the disintegration of

---

52 Bush (1990).

53 Wheeler (2002).

54 UN Security Council (1991).

the Eastern Bloc in Europe and the increasing amount of transnational conflicts in Africa, Boutros Ghali brought about a proposal for an increased efficiency of UN decision-making in times of immediate crisis. In *An Agenda for Peace* (1992) Boutros Ghali addressed the threats that were posed by civil conflicts, humanitarian disasters and state collapse. As the UN involvement in crisis in the early 1990s was mainly characterized by traditional peacekeeping operations, posing "[...] little threat to norms of international sovereignty and territorial integrity because they serve with the consent of all parties and play a non-coercive role [...]",[55] Boutros Ghali knew that with the growing complexity of intra-state conflicts, peacekeeping operations in the traditional sense would not be sufficient anymore to meet the requirements. Traditional peacekeeping defined by a strict post-conflict operation with limited or no coercive character had to be gradually reformed to become peace enforcement missions, which were to be deployed in crisis regions prior to a *de facto* peace agreement and equipped with a mandate allowing for coercive action if necessary.[56] In *An Agenda for Peace* Boutros Ghali refers to the changing nature of conflict through the erosion of national boundaries by new communication technology and global commercial links.[57] Describing the current times as times of global transition, Boutros Ghali creates an image of a globalized world in which poverty, disease and famine produce refugee flows that pose a destabilizing threat to international peace and security.[58] In order to increase the efficiency and responsiveness of the UN system in addressing these threats, Boutros Ghali introduces a new instrument of conflict resolution, which may be used as a means of last resort to solve a conflict: peace-enforcement.[59]Although Boutros Ghali does not make an explicit reference to the term humanitarian intervention, the strategy of peace-enforcement or peacemaking comes close to the coercive character of humanitarian intervention enforcing peace on the belligerent parties. Thereby, Boutros Ghali compromises the notion of exclusive and absolute sovereignty behind which leaders can hide from persecution. Under point 17, Boutros Ghali declares that

> [...] the time of absolute and exclusive sovereignty, however, has passed; its theory was never matched by reality. It is the task of leaders of States today to understand this and to find a balance between the needs of good internal governance and the requirements of an ever more interdependent world [...].[60]

Boutros Ghali picks up the aspect of good internal governance later on in the report and for the first time draws the connection between state sovereignty over domestic affairs and the state responsibility to care for well-being of its citizens. Boutros Ghali asserts that the sovereignty of Member States is respected when in

---

55 Ottaway and Lacina (2003).

56 Boulden (2001).

57 The United Nations Secretary General (1992).

58 Ibid (p.3).

59 Ibid (p.5).

60 Ibid (p.4).

turn the Member States live up to their "[...] responsibility [...] to take care of the victims of emergencies occurring on their territory [...]".[61] Stating the possibility of a deployment of highly armed and well-trained peace enforcement units in countries reluctant to cooperate with UN conflict resolution instruments, the signals sent out by the secretary general were to be understood as a *de facto* relaxation of the sovereignty principle when used as a shield to protect regimes of internal injustice. The concept of peace-enforcement for the first time in the UN history envisaged a possibility for the UN to coercively enforce cease-fire agreements.[62] Regardless of the fact that the contemporary concept of humanitarian intervention was not fully established, yet, the *Agenda for Peace* sets the foundation for the later developed 'responsibility to protect'.

Despite Boutros Ghali's ambitious attempt to revolutionize the effectiveness of the UN system in face of immanent crisis, his leadership was overshadowed by the UN's failure to act during the Rwandan genocide in 1994. The experience of 18 killed US soldiers during the humanitarian intervention in Somalia a year earlier had triggered a Western attitude of by-standing as hundreds of thousands of people were killed during one of the most severe genocides in history.[63] The humanitarian catastrophe of Rwanda called for a widespread reform of the UN system and its legal commitment to the possibility to intervene into the domestic affairs of another state. In the aftermath of Rwanda the international community could finally agree in July 1998 to establish an International Criminal Court able to hold individuals responsible for their violations of human rights law, war crimes, crimes against humanity and the crime of aggression.

The ratification of the Rome Statute establishing the International Criminal Court (ICC) marks another important corner stone in the evolution of the UN system from a purely Westphalian model to a system where the sovereignty of a nation state is dependent on its internal governance. While in the orthodox interpretation of sovereignty the ruler of a country *est imperator in regno suo,*[64] the establishment of the ICC limits the unrestricted autonomy and sovereignty of the ruler since the ICC has the legal power to hold individuals responsible for their criminal acts under international law. "[...] A person who commits a crime within the jurisdiction of the Court shall be individually responsible and liable for punishment in accordance with this Statute [...]".[65] By allowing the persecution and conviction of individual decision makers for crimes under international law, the Rome Statute strongly interferes with the sovereignty of the particular state. Taking away state sovereignty as a shield behind which individual decision makers could hide, meant that decades of impunity were formally about to come

---

[61] Ibid (p.8).

[62] Ottaway and Lacina Op. Cit. 56 (p. 77).

[63] Grünfeld (2007).

[64] Canning (2003).

[65] United Nations General Assembly (1998).

to an end.[66] The ICC Statute constitutes another decisive step away from interstate justice to individual justice for the benefit of individuals under attack by their own government. Thereby, the Rome Statute makes a clear statement in favour of the precedence of individual rights over the rights of states by expanding the court's jurisdiction beyond the boundaries of the sovereignty principle.[67]

The rather minor changes in the nature of the UN's legal system brought about in the 1990 s fall short in really revolutionizing the system so as to strengthen the rights of individuals *vis-à-vis* the rights of states. Since the experience of the Rwandan genocide scholars have pushed the UN to adapt the legal base of the international community to the changing realities in the post-1990 world. The *de jure* exclusive and absolute sovereignty principle was identified as the main impediment for the UN to effectively address crises that were regarded as falling outside the international peace and security realm. The UN needed a new concept of collective security transgressing the conventionally-perceived dichotomy between state sovereignty and the security of the people living in this state. The reason is that "[...] unlimited sovereignty, not restrained by respect for law and human dignity and freedom, leads [...] domestically to widespread oppression [...]".[68] A broad consensus emerged that sovereignty should not only be circumcised in case the state poses an external threat to neighbouring countries but foremost when it fails to protect its own citizens or in other words falls short in providing the state's protection for certain groups of people. The term of collective security has to be extended from its foreign relations dimension to its domestic dimension, i.e. the collective right and duty to enforce protection of citizens. Failed states, characterized by *bad government* such as Rwanda or Somalia, have to be reminded by the international community that it is their duty to uphold human rights and freedoms. If they are not able to provide these basic duties, the UN should call for collective intervention to assist the state to meet its duties.[69] Hence, scholars such as Evans stated that while states have a right of sovereignty, they also have a duty that arises from this right, namely the moral duty of every state to provide for the wellbeing of its citizens, i.e. "[...] the duty to protect communities from mass killing, women from systematic rape, and children from starvation [...]".[70] It follows, if states fail to do justice to their responsibility to protect its people, the international community has to take over the role of the state and guarantee the protection of human beings. Thus, when a population is suffering serious harm as result of insurgency, internal war, repression or state failure and the state in power is either unwilling or unable to halt or avert these atrocities from happening, the protection of every individual state's sovereignty can be compromised.[71]

---

66 Scharf (1998).

67 United Nations Secretariat (2004).

68 Hieronymi (1996).

69 Ibid (p.239).

70 Evans and Sahnoun (2002).

71 Ibid (p.102).

Following the scholarly debate about the effects of the conditionality of sovereignty in case a state fails to meet its duty to protect its citizens, an International Commission on Intervention and State Sovereignty (ICISS) was established in 2000. Within a year the ICISS filed a report that officially introduced the principle of the 'responsibility to protect'(R2P), which interprets the sovereignty principle as laid down in Art. 2 (1) UN primarily as a responsibility for the protection of its own people.[72] This responsibility to protect creates conditionality for the sovereignty principle as the report authorizes and even urges the international community to intervene in situations where states fail to fulfil their obligation.

> [...] Where a population is suffering serious harm, as a result of internal war, insurgency, repression or state failure, and the state in question is unwilling or unable to halt or avert it, the principle of non-intervention yields to the international responsibility to protect [...].[73]

According to the ICISS Report the official recognition of the duty to commit to individual justice would allow the international community to consistently intervene in situations of gross, large scale loss of life and/or large scale ethnic cleansing. Only if mediation, embargos or any kind of diplomatic pressure fail to bring states to the execution of its duties, the ICISS Report states that the international community does not only have the right but also the responsibility to act and not watch passively as a bystander. The primary purpose of these interventions must be to bring human suffering to a halt.[74]

The Report of the UN High-level Panel on Threats, Challenges and Change (HLPR) from 2004 continues where the ICISS Report left off by setting up coherent guidelines on basis of the 'R2P' that address every organ of the UN. The HLPR officially adopts the 'responsibility to protect' in the context of Chapter VII of the UN Charter. The HLPR criticises the current UN Charter system for failing to equip the Security Council with the rights to authorize military interventions in cases domestic humanitarian atrocities. Since the UN system *de facto* only legitimizes the Security Council to take action to restore international peace and security and not to intervene in internal affairs of a sovereign state, the HLPR urges the UN to take the necessary steps in order to broaden the Security Council's competences when it comes to providing relief for individuals in man-made catastrophes that are officially internal matters. According to the HLPR the extension of the Security Council's competences can be justified on basis of the Genocide Convention.[75] The HLPR explicitly states that the genocide in Rwanda, the crimes against humanity in Kosovo, Darfur, Bosnia and Herzegovina and Somalia were able to occur because of the inflexibility to intervene in reliance to Art. 2 (7) of the UN Charter. According to the HLPR, state sovereignty should be bound to conditionality, i.e. the responsibility to protect all citizens on its territory.

---

72 ICISS (2001).

73 Ibid (p.IX).

74 Ibid (p.17).

75 UN Secretariat Op. Cit. 68(p.65).

> [...] Sovereign governments have the primary responsibility to protect their own citizens from such catastrophes, when they are unable or unwilling to do so that responsibility should be taken up by the wider international community [...].[76]

In line with the ICISS Report, the HLPR affirms that the international community must not shrink back from using military force as a means of last resort to protect human beings from large scale suffering in case of a humanitarian emergency. Thereby, the HLPR and the ICISS try to extend the scope of the legal imperative to intervene in cases of genocide arising from the Genocide Convention to crimes against humanity, war crimes and other violations of international humanitarian law.

The United Nations have adopted the guidelines of the concept as established by the ICISS and the HLPR into the 2005 World Summit Outcome Document where it has been stated once again under point 139 that

> [...] The international community, through the United Nations, also has the responsibility to use appropriate diplomatic, humanitarian and other peaceful means, in accordance with Chapters VI and VIII of the Charter, to help protect populations from genocide, war crimes, ethnic cleansing and crimes against humanity.[77]

Following the declaration that the international community has the responsibility to take all peaceful measures to make perpetrating states comply with their duty, point 139 also envisages the use of coercive measures to save individuals.

> [...] In this context, we are prepared to take collective action [...] through the Security Council [...] on a case-by-case basis and in cooperation with relevant regional organizations as appropriate, should peaceful means be inadequate and national authorities manifestly fail to protect their populations from genocide, war crimes, ethnic cleansing and crimes against humanity [...].[78]

This notion is being picked again by the Security Council in April 2006 and integrated into SC Resolution 1674 (2006) that reaffirms "[...] the provisions of paragraphs 138 and 139 of the 2005 World Summit Outcome Document regarding the responsibility to protect populations from genocide, war crimes, ethnic cleansing and crimes against humanity [...]".[79] Thereby the Security Council declares that it is committed to take action to protect civilians in armed conflict and to intervene into internal matters of sovereign states that fail to fulfil their duty of protecting their own people.

The responsibility to protect is the result of the evolution of international law in the 1990s. Formally, the UN system as it stands today, accepts the humanitarian rationale of intervention as a mean of last resort in face of an acute humanitarian emergency. The preservation of the sovereignty principle in codified law and the ambiguity of the formulation of the responsibility to protect, however, leave the

---

[76] Ibid (p.66).

[77] UN General Assembly (2005).

[78] Ibid (p.31).

[79] UN Security Council (2006).

states the freedom to decide when to intervene unless the crisis at hand has been classified as genocide. As a result, the responsibility to protect up until today has not managed to establish a coherent approach to humanitarian crises regardless of the type of crime committed.

1.3 The Ethics of Humanitarian Intervention

1.3.1 Intervention in Just War Theory

Having focused on the legality of intervention in the previous sub-chapter, this sub-chapter will focus on the moral and ethical legitimacy of intervention from the perspective of normative just war theory. For millennia the concept of the use of force has been highly debated and the criteria for a *bellum justum* have been constantly redefined. Particularly in centuries characterised by an absence of a legal codex the moral interpretation of a just war has been the only constraint on the use of force.

"[…] The name just war stands for a broad and consensually shaped tradition in Western culture on the problems of justifying and restraining the violence of war […]".[80] Just war describes a moral debate that is rooted in the philosophical writings of the Antiquity and that is concerned with the morality of warfare. Not only does just war theory focus on the decision to go to war (*jus ad bellum*) but also on the righteous conduct of warfare during the war (*jus in bello*).[81] In this book I will only focus on the *jus ad bellum*, i.e. the criteria that make the use of force just and the cause of the war legitimate. From a modern Western perspective the debate concerning the morality of the use of force is highly controversial due to the fact that in particular Western Judaeo-Christian values frown upon violence as a means of social interaction. Thus, the term of a 'just war' creates a similar oxymoron as 'humanitarian intervention'. As Kurt Tucholsky once stated "[…] There can be no such thing as a just war […]".[82] Tucholsky's statement makes a valid point bearing in mind that war always features violence, death and human suffering. However, looking at the history of human interaction, war appears to be a constant companion of human activity. Therefore, settling for the second best, namely the acceptance of the use of force under certain restrictions, might be the only option to deal with the anarchic nature of the international arena.[83]

Even though early references to just war can be found in secular writings of Ancient Greek and Roman literature, the actual link between the use of force and moral justice finds its roots in the birth of monotheistic religion since both concepts religion and warfare were always closely interrelated and used together.

---

80 Johnson (1984).

81 Fixdal and Smith (1998.

82 Kurt Tucholsky cited by Nicolaus (2003).

83 Helmke Op. Cit. 7 (p. 10).

In Judaism and Jewish traditions warfare was subject to both a quasi *ius in bello* and a *ius ad bellum*. In the Thora and in the Talmud two types of wars were distinguished: a *milhemet hova* (obligatory war) and a *milhemet reshut* (an optional war). While a defensive war is not only a right but an obligatory duty, expansionist wars were optional and could only be justified when fought against peoples not adhering to the Noahide laws and thereby threatening the religious integrity of the Israelites.[84] Much stronger than the optional war is however the reference to the obligatory war of self-defence that is referred to in Exodus 22:1: "If someone comes to kill you, kill him first". Judaism both in religious and secular terms laid down the foundation for a concept of a *bellum justum* in case of self-defence.

With the Christian Church becoming an institutionalized organization of power in the late Roman Empire and realizing that political power and religion could no longer be separated, Christian notions of the use of force merged with the Roman legal traditions of a *bellum justum*. As one of the first Christian writers combining Roman traditions of a *bellum justum* and the Christian value of love one's fellowman, Saint Augustine of Hippo who lived in the 5th century addressed the issue of engaging in hostilities for a just cause. While it would be certainly overstated to claim that Augustine was an early realist, he nonetheless realized that idealist Christian values of pacifism were not compatible with the real world. Therefore, Augustine in *City of God* tries to replace Christian pacifism with a more realist approach to world affairs without disregarding the aspect of ethics. Experiencing the final days of Rome before its destruction, Augustine lost most of its idealism observing the sinfulness of human nature, which makes the use of force a necessary evil in a drive for self-preservation. Nonetheless, the necessity of the use of force does not compromise the necessity of man's actions to be virtuous. Consequently, the waging of a war by a virtuous man has to be a just war.[85] Convinced of the fact that the nature of mankind is prone to make use of violence while in the same time trying to emphasise the importance of virtue, Augustine sits "[…] on the cusp between realism and idealism, seeking the virtuous path through a sinful world […]".[86] According to Augustine the justice in war derives from three fundamental criteria: just cause, right intent and lawful authority. Based on the first criterion war must only be waged if the cause of the war is just, i.e. if the war breaks out in order to restore peace. Further, particularly the motive for responding to the cause of war have to be just, namely one must not be driven by the love of violence or the lust of power. Finally, only a legitimate authority may declare war.[87] Apart from the expressed adherence to interstate justice, Augustine also refers to the importance of individual justice and the necessity of rulers to launch wars first and foremost for the sake of assisting human beings in need. This conviction stemming from religious ethics of charity links the concept of right

---

84 Solomon (2005).

85 Augustine of Hippo St. (1984).

86 Fixdal and Smith (1998) Op. Cit. 82 (p.287).

87 Bjorna Op. Cit. 38 (p. 22).

intent with the well-being of individuals and paves the way for war on basis of humanitarian considerations.[88]

On basis of the criteria set out by Augustine in the 5th century, the Christian priest Thomas Aquinas formulated his theory of a just war in the 13th century based on the law of nature. The law of nature is rooted in Roman law and philosophy and can be defined as

> [...] right reason in harmony with nature, it is of universal application, unchanging and everlasting, it summons to duty by its commands, and averts from wrongdoing by its prohibitions [...] we cannot be freed from its obligations by senate or people, and we need not look outside ourselves for an expounder or interpreter of it [...][89]

That is to say, that the natural law is a theory arguing that certain rights and obligations in international society derive from the virtue of common humanity. This natural doctrine is not to be altered and has universal application for mankind as it is God given and inherent in human nature.[90] For Aquinas natural law is the application of the divine law by human rulers and underlies the basic principle that "[...] good is to be done and pursued, and evil is to be avoided [...]".[91] Thus, Aquinas' perception of the world was based on a typical Medieval Catholic good-bad divide. The goodness or virtuosity of an action has to be assessed on basis of the intention of the action taker. Even though Aquinas adopts the three basic Augustinian criteria for a just war, from Aquinas' viewpoint the supreme criterion on basis of which one is to assess the justness of a war is the criterion of the right intention. The only intent that may be accepted, according to Aquinas, is the motive of just peace, excluding self-interested motives like profit, power and glory.[92] As these criteria are religious ones, actual ulterior self-interested motives other than peace will be judged not by an earthly jury but will be judged by God and should therefore be avoided. Translated into political reality, Aquinas only accepted the use of force as an act of self-defence since according to the law of nature mankind is impregnated by a rational drive of self-preservation. Therefore, Aquinas regarded war just if it was waged for defensive reasons in order to preserve one's existence. This rationale derives from Aquinas' justification of killing as an unfortunate and unintended result of an act of self-defence.[93]

Hugo Grotius picks up the theories of Augustine and Aquinas in the 17th century shortly after the 30 years war and fuses them into a theory that goes beyond the purely Christian religious approach of his ancestors. The experience of the devastating war between Catholics and Protestants in Central Europe and the following Peace of Westphalia had transformed the ideology of many scholars of the time from a religiously loaded to a more secular, state-focused one. Based on

---

88 Mednicoff (2006).

89 Cicero (1928).

90 Holzgrefe and Keohane (2003).

91 Aquinas (1947).

92 Fixdal and Smith (1998) Op. Cit. 82 (p.299).

93 Bjorna Op. Cit. 38 (p. 23).

Aquinas' assumption of a natural law of common humanity, Grotius developed a theory embracing both fundamental Christian values of virtuous conduct such as charity, compassion, moderation as well as modesty with a more secular notion of sovereignty. Grotius envisaged a post-Westphalian world in which the rule of law could coexist with a moral pretension of virtuosity.[94] Grounded in natural law, human kind was believed to be defined by a set of natural dispositions such as sympathize with others, fulfil promises, act in accordance with general principles of humanity, use language and inflict penalties for wrongdoings. These natural dispositions could according to Grotius not only be attributed to individuals but also to states, which had to be constrained by a set of rules that could be enforced if necessary. Grotius considers three main valid causes for a just war within an international system that exists within the realm of fairness and justice: self-defence, restitution and punishment.[95] As natural rights were understood to be universal, and sympathy as well as empathy with your neighbour were considered to be inherent values of this law of nature, intervention and punishment could be considered legitimate as long as they were serving the common interests of humanity. In that sense Grotius did not regard the principle of the ruler's sovereignty exclusive and unconditional; in fact Grotius stated that if a ruler mistreated his subjects launching a war to oust this ruler was legitimate. Grotius stated that

> [...] If, however, the wrong is obvious, in case some [tyrant] should inflict upon his subject such treatment as no one is warranted in inflicting, the exercise of the right vested in human society is not precluded [...].[96]

Grotius continues by saying that

> [...] Yet where a Busiris, a Phalaris or a Thracian Diomede provoke their people to despair and resistance by unheard of cruelties, having themselves abandoned all the laws of nature, they lose the rights of independent sovereigns, and can no longer claim the privilege of the law of nations [...].[97]

What Grotius established here already in 1625 comes close to the contemporary debate in international law transforming sovereignty from an exclusive right into a conditional responsibility. Further, Grotius advances a set of six criteria that have to be met in order to be able to classify a forceful intervention as a just war. A just war has to be fought for a just cause such as to redress an injury to the state; it has to be proportionate to the ends to be achieved; it should offer a reasonable chance of success; it requires a public declaration of war; it has to be fought by a right authority; and finally it has to be an act of last resort. These criteria make Grotius' work an important cornerstone for the concept of a legal and legitimate war in international law and in Just War Theory.[98]

---

[94] Mednicoff Op. Cit. 89 (p.379).

[95] Bjorna Op. Cit. 38(p. 24).

[96] Chesterman (2003).

[97] Grotius (2001).

[98] Bjorna Op. Cit. 38 (p. 24).

Contemporary Just War Theory is divided in several distinct traditions or schools of thought, that derive from the historic roots of Augustine, Aquinas and Grotius and that address the use of force in international relations differently. These distinctions evolve around the core issue of *jus ad bellum* as the trade-off between state justice and individual justice, namely the question whether a just war is based on primarily satisfying the right of states or the right of individuals.

Statism is one of the most conservative models and originates in Machiavelli's state model that describes the state as the most important actor in international relations. State sovereignty is the paramount principle in this model, granting the state the freedom to decide to what extent individuals residing in its territory enjoy individual rights. In this absolute state-centric tradition violations of the sovereignty principle emerge only as a form of power politics and not as a form of humanitarian concern. That is to say, that any infringement of state sovereignty occurs as a result of a state's ambition to extend its influence and power. The right to intervene into the domestic affairs of another state is perceived as deriving from the mere ability to do so, i.e. the weaker states are naturally exposed to the will of the stronger.[99]

Internationalism has to be considered a more progressive model since it moves away from the statist Machiavellian model towards a tradition corresponding with Grotius' theory. Even though the state is regarded the most important actor in the international arena, its sovereignty must not be regarded exclusive and unconditional as the rights of individuals become a matter of international concern in cases when human rights norms are completely disregarded by the respective government.[100] Internationalism as a model that occurred only in recent decades tries to incorporate the growing internationalization of politics through the creation of international regimes, however, does not disregard the persisting power of international law that is based on a rather statist model. The reason being that the enforcement of a *de facto* right of intervention for human rights, still requires the consent of the nation state, thereby making the solidarist nature of human rights bound to the statist nature of the system.[101]

Cosmopolitanism goes even a step further by characterizing the international system as a community of individuals and only secondarily as a community of states. States only receive rights if they promote the rights and the welfare of individuals.[102] Reisman (1990) even goes so far as to define the sovereignty principle as the people's rather than the sovereign's sovereignty.[103] In the eyes of a cosmopolitan the major question in international relations and conflict has to be how to meet the needs of the world's citizens. The notion of a common humanity and the idea to intervene for the sake of the protection of human beings in

---

[99] Donnelly (1995).

[100] Ibid (p.121).

[101] Greenwood (1993).

[102] McCarthey (1993).

[103] Reisman (1990).

cosmopolitanism stems from early just war theorists such as Augustine who defined a just war as an act of charity to the well being of people.[104] Cosmopolitans take a rather egalitarianism approach to international relations that pushes for an equal moral consideration of all individuals worldwide. Concepts of race, nationality or gender are not deemed important.[105] Hence, a forceful intervention into a state, serving the purpose of enhancing the wellbeing of individuals, is considered just by cosmopolitans.

Corresponding with the ideas brought forward by cosmopolitans is the model of *Solidarism* in international relations. Solidarism is based on the concept of a world above or beyond national borders defined by common humanity. "[...] Solidarism represents a high degree of shared norms, rules and institutions between states in the international environment, where the focus is on cooperation rather than coexistence [...]".[106] Even though solidarism regards both state sovereignty and human rights as equally important norms, the sovereignty principle is usually understood to be dependent on the human rights record of the country. Solidarism as well as other cosmopolitan theories places the human being rather than the state at the centre of the international system and the centre of their study. Thus, in solidarism the governments are responsible for the protection of human rights and civilians under threat at home and abroad. This responsibility of governments also includes putting their own nationals at risk to save victims of gross human rights violations abroad due to the fact that there is no distinction between one's own nationals and strangers; the world is comprised of a common humanity.[107] In Wheeler's (2002) solidarist belief a just war or a just intervention has to be based on four paramount criteria related to the criteria laid down by scholars of earlier periods. First of all, states must intervene for a just cause. A just cause has to be a supreme humanitarian emergency,[108] only existing when the fate of the to be protected community depends on the intervention of outsiders such as in the cases of crimes against humanity, genocide, massive expulsion, displacement of people, state breakdown leading to famine or mass murder. Secondly, a just intervention must come as a means of last resort after all other means of conflict resolution have been exhausted.[109] Thirdly, interventions have to meet the proportionality principle, which means that the means used have to be proportionate to the desired ends.

---

[104] Pastor (1993).

[105] Holzgrefe and Keohane Op. Cit. 91 (p. 20).

[106] Welin (2005).

[107] Wheeler (2002).

[108] Wheeler picks up the concept of the supreme emergency from Walzer who defines a supreme emergency as a situation where a country victimized by aggression is about to be defeated militarily and is threatened by the prospect of the aggressor instituting a brutal regime of massacre and enslavement against individuals of the defeated nation. A supreme humanitarian emergency is a state of emergency arising from human rights abuses that are that severe that they shock the conscience of mankind and which to stop requires the intervention of an external party. [See Walzer (2006)].

[109] Rodley (1992).

Finally, a just intervention has to be accompanied by a reasonable chance of success, which will be assessed on basis of the produced humanitarian outcome, namely whether the intervention has rescued victims of oppression, and whether human rights have subsequently been restored.[110]

Humanism, too, is founded on the cosmopolitan belief of a common humanity arising from common human history. However, unlike solidarism or natural law theories, humanism does not allow for the use of force under any circumstances due to the fact that any use of violence, force and certainly war is inherently evil and brings about the most evil in mankind. Humanism derives from the Christian moral conception that human beings are brothers and that hence any form of warfare would come close to fratricide.[111] Erasmus, one of the most prominent humanist writers, laid down in his work *The Complaint of Peace* 1517 that war is utterly opposed to the ideals of Christianity and that war "[...] overturns all our best hopes, leaving us in the foul sink of sin as well as misery [...]".[112] Therefore, pacifism is the only solution to a struggling world. Humanism foresees the erection of a world-embracing central regulatory system including all important powers based on a common constitution with the sole purpose of ensuring a peaceful world. This confederation of states has to have a strong judicial and executive body at its disposal in order to assure that norms are enforceable and in turn states will be held liable for provisions that are legally binding. Thereby, this confederation of states will go beyond a mere intergovernmental organization and become an organization with a strong supranational institution making the compliance with international decisions compulsory. Further, humanism envisages a total prohibition of the use of force under all circumstances in view of the fact that any conditional permission for the use of force facilitates its abuse.[113]

Unlike the traditions presented above *Utilitarianism* is not founded on the idea of a cosmopolitan world where common humanity requires solidarity or charitable action in order to enhance the well-being of your fellow man. Utilitarianism is closely related to a rational choice approach where the maximization of benefit, in this case utility, is the prime motivation for individuals and states. In the utilitarian doctrine an action is considered just if the consequences are more favourable than unfavourable to all parties. Conduct in itself or even the cause of an action cannot be good or bad, as the moral value of an action derives from the goodness or badness of the outcome.[114] The utilitarian school divides into two traditions that approach the concept of utility differently. On the one hand there are act-utilitarians who solely focus on the immediate outcome of a certain action while disregarding norms or rules. On the other hand there rule-utilitarians believe that overall human welfare is best provided for if all actors adhere to the given norms

---

110 Wheeler (2002).

111 Skinner (1978).

112 Erasmus (1917).

113 Bjorna Op. Cit. 38 (p. 25–26).

114 Holzgrefe and Keohane (2003) Op. Cit. 91 (p. 20).

and rules. The former hold that each human action is an object of close moral evaluation that implies that a certain action is just if its direct and immediate consequences increase the aggregate utility of all. Thus, for act-utilitarians the justness of a war or intervention depends entirely on its consequences. An intervention for humanitarian purposes for example is considered just if it saves more lives than it costs or unjust if it costs more lives than it saves. The sole adherence to the maximization of aggregate utility or well-being, however, might become controversial once it justifies "[...] the sacrifice of human rights of a vulnerable group for the sake of the greater satisfaction or happiness of a small privileged elite or a large but already relatively privileged group [...]" .[115] Hence, act-utilitarianism would allow self-interested interventions that would enable the economic exploitation of a country for the sake of cheap raw materials generating a great overall utility or great utility for the intervener. Jeremy Bentham, however, criticizes act-utilitarianism for allowing intervention that would relieve the suffering of foreign nationals and increase aggregate utility, but decrease utility for the intervening nation. A "[...] nation should refuse to render positive services to a foreign nation, when the rendering of them would produce more good to the last-mentioned nation, than would produce evil to itself [...]".[116]

Rule-Utilitarians on the contrary do not solely base their assessment of the justness of an intervention on the consequences of the intervention but believe that actions generate the highest aggregate utility if all actors follow the rules that have been agreed upon by the community.

> [...] Often the only way to maximize the utility that arises from my act is by knowing (or guess) what others are likely to do [...] The best way of coordinating or actions with those of others, and thereby to maximize, [...] is to promulgate rules (themselves chosen with an eye to maximizing utility, of course) and to adhere to them [...].[117]

The reasoning behind this argument is that only in a world where all actors can rely on and predict the actions of the fellow actors, stability can arise that will enhance economic and social prospering. In terms of humanitarian intervention, unfortunately, rule-utilitarians have not found a rule that equally satisfies all parties concerned. The failure of humanitarian intervention has mostly been traced back to the lack of a rule that is able to secure the best consequences for all parties concerned.[118]

1.3.2 The Criterion of 'Right intention'

Apart from pacifism that rejects the use of force in its entirety, all other models of just war theory have accepted the fact that in certain scenarios the use of force may

---

[115] Garrett (2004).

[116] Bentham (1962).

[117] Goodin (1995).

[118] Holzgrefe and Keohane (2003) Op. Cit. 91 (p. 24).

within limits be justifiable. Looking at the various traditions in just war theory and the criteria that have been brought forward to define an ethically justified use of force, the decisive factor in determining the justness of a war seems to be the right intention. Humanitarian intervention as the only legally tolerated form of intervention into the domestic affairs of another state requires this criterion to be satisfied. Despite the existence of additional criteria that have legitimizing authority for intervention, the main debate in just war theory evolves around the question of whether motive or outcome matters.[119]

As both the term intention and motivation are commonly used interchangeably, it becomes imperative to define the two terms that both point in the same direction but describe two different concepts. It is worth noting that just war theory usually uses the term right intention as one of its prime criteria for legitimizing the use of force. The actual motivation of the actor is mostly disregarded. Nardin (2006) categorises intentions as the "[…] state of affairs it seeks to bring about. A motive, in contrast, is the frame of mind in which agents act—the desires and other passions that propel him […]".[120] In other words an intention describes what the actor wants to achieve disregarding the question of why he wants to achieve it. The motive, however, is the actual driving force behind the action, a further goal that one wishes to accomplish with the intended act.[121] Saving a drowning kitten solely because I expect to receive a reward from the owner makes my intention right (rescuing the kitten) while my motive is self-interested as I am expecting a reward.[122] According to just war theory the 'right intention' is a prerequisite for a just intervention, while the issue of 'right motivation' is rarely addressed. The reason for that might be that measuring motives or ulterior motives of actions is close to impossible, while the intention may be more obvious. In order to assess the driving force for governments to intervene in certain crises it is necessary to shed light on both aspects of decision making.[123]

As noted, Augustine stressed the point that killing or waging a war can only be considered just if it is carried out with the right intent, namely putting an end to a grave injustice or restoring peace.[124] That is to say, for Augustine the intention of going to war must be filled by the desire for peace, the advancement of good, securing of peace, punishment of evildoers, or the avoidance of evil. Feelings of vengeance, fever of revolt are unconditionally rejected.[125] While Augustine does not make a clear distinction between intent and motive, thereby ignoring the possibility of the existence of ulterior motives, Verwey goes beyond the mere right intent by stating in addition that humanitarian interventions need to be motivated

[119] Bellamy (2004).
[120] Nardin (2006).
[121] Teson (2005).
[122] Dobos (2008).
[123] Seay (2007).
[124] Bellamy Op. Cit. 120 (p. 227).
[125] Bjorna (2009) Op. Cit. 38 (p. 36).

by "[...] the sole purpose of preventing or putting a halt to [...]"[126] a humanitarian crisis. According to Verwey's definition humanitarian interventions should be entirely or primarily driven not only by a humanitarian intent but also by a humanitarian motivation of the intervener, e.g. promoting the welfare of suffering citizens as well as in the same time preventing or halting a humanitarian catastrophe.[127] Verwey (1992) has defined humanitarian intervention narrowly as an action solely driven by a humanitarian motivation. Therefore, looking at the Cold War period, Verwey has difficulties finding any real humanitarian interventions since there was always an ulterior, self-seeking and power serving motivation underlying superpower interventions.[128] Throughout the 1990s, many writers gradually stepped away from this narrow definition of a morally right purpose of humanitarian intervention, based on both intent and motive. In a more lenient way a just intervention was defined by Parekh as an "[...] act wholly or primarily guided by the sentiment of humanity, compassion or fellow-feeling and in that sense disinterested [...]".[129] Even though humanity and compassion with your fellow man are to dominate the motivation to intervene, Parekh's interpretation recognizes that it might not be necessarily the sole driving force to intervention. Apart from that, Parekh suggests that the intervention should be 'disinterested' to an extent that the humanitarian aspect of intervention does not become a mere by-product of an otherwise rather self-interested intervention. Here, Parekh's interpretation correlates with Aquinas' double-effect argument that holds that the action is just as long as the injustice of the unjust effect does not outweigh the justness of the just effect.[130] Thomas Aquinas is one of the first just war theorists mentioning the double effect, a reality that appears quite frequently in international affairs. Thomas Aquinas recognizes that in reality one intention might not come alone and is most likely accompanied by secondary side-effects of different nature.

> [...] Nothing hinders one act from having two effects, only one of which is intended, while the other is beside the intention. [...] Accordingly the act of self-defense may have two effects, one is the saving of one's own life, the other is the slaying of the aggressor. Therefore, this act, since one's intention is to save one's own life, is not unlawful [...][131].

Thus, according to Aquinas an action might have two effects, one is intended and the other is a mere unintended side-effect. The one taking the life has to demonstrate that his intent was the one of self-preservation. Translated into international relations, that is to say that governments have to demonstrate that their intent is to promote common good. Ramsey (1986) defines four conditions that have to be met in order to define an intention as good. First of all, the desired end must be good in itself. Secondly, the good effect and not the evil effect must be intended.

---

126 Verwey (1992) cited in Malanczuk (1993).

127 Verwey (1992).

128 Ibid (p.114 ff.).

129 Parekh (1997).

130 Bellamy AJ Op. Cit. 120 (p. 223).

131 Ramsey (1986).

Thirdly, the good effect must not be produced as a side-effect of the evil and finally the good of the good effect must outweigh the evil of the evil effect.[132] Thus, even though a side-effect of an action might come about regardless of the intent and motivation of the action taker, it nonetheless has an impact on the actual purpose of intervention.

Following this definition of humanitarian intervention, when a state intervenes into a humanitarian crisis having humanitarian ends as its intention, but has ulterior motives, the intervention is to be morally and ethically rejected. Thus, some scholars argue for a disinterested intervention on the principle that humanitarianism must imply a certain degree of altruistic or charitable motivation. Others call for impartiality in humanitarian intervention by arguing that allowing for self-interested humanitarian intervention would endanger the concept and its effectiveness. The narrow understanding of humanitarianism is founded on the ICRC's[133] four key principles: humanity, impartiality, neutrality and universality. This conservative approach to the concept of humanitarian intervention sets out the same standards for military state intervention into humanitarian crisis as for humanitarian intervention by charitable NGOs, resembling traditional ideas of humanitarianism.[134] Namely, an intervention that is motivated by the self-interest of the intervener might raise the fear in the receiving state that the intervener is actually interested in undermining the local power relations for its own purposes and not in order to save individuals. To be exact, in order to preserve the weak international consensus that intervention for humanitarian purposes may be an exception to the non-intervention principle, humanitarian intervention must not receive the reputation that it may be a Trojan horse for foreign interveners to gain control over domestic affairs in the target country.[135]

> [...] The fact that in the present international system those with the resources to intervene are former colonial powers or large and traditionally obtrusive neighbours does not facilitate the discussion [...].[136]

In particular the concept of national interests, which is closely connected in political science to realist power maximization theory, is rejected in its entirety not only as a just intention but also as a righteous motivation. The main argument behind the refutation of a self-interested motivation for intervention, is that it will lead in the long-term to a steady abuse of a concept that inherently ought to be concerned with saving individuals.[137]

Realist theory, founded on the belief that states are rational actors and always follow self-interested motivations, might argue that the entire concept of an

132 Ibid (p. 49).

133 ICRC = The International Committee of the Red Cross.

134 Ramsbotham and Woodhouse (1996).

135 Leifer Leifer (1993).

136 Chopra and Weiss (1992).

137 Ryter (2003) Op. Cit. 17 (p.26).

intervention for altruistic purposes is unrealistic in a world of self-seeking actors. As Pogge (2006) stated "[...] there are no humanitarian heroes out there [...]".[138] On the contrary, liberalists might argue that humanitarian intervention is defined by its intention not by its motivation.[139] Even though it should be an ideal goal for interveners to synchronize motives and intention, so as to let both be primarily guided by humanitarian ends, realists argue that one might want to arrange oneself with the fact that in the real world multiple motives for the intervention into humanitarian crisis are unavoidable. Therefore, above all the intention of the intervener, not the motivation, should be taken as a measure of the humanitarian nature of an intervention, i.e. of the justness of the intervention. Ulterior motives

> [...] do not necessarily count against the morality of the intervention [...] the true test is whether the intervention has put an end to human rights deprivations. That is sufficient to meet the requirement of disinterestedness, even if there are other non-humanitarian reasons behind the intervention [...] it follows that, even if an intervention is motivated by non-humanitarian reasons, it can still count as humanitarian provided that the motives, and the means employed, do not undermine a positive humanitarian outcome [...].[140]

Hence, based on Teson, an intervention might still be called righteous if the outcome of the intervention serves the humanitarian interest of the international community despite the motives being potentially self-interested. Thereby, Teson takes a utilitarian approach stating that the justness of humanitarian interventions has to be assessed on basis of the consequences produced, namely the effects the intervention had for the people on the ground.

Despite the fact that the scholarly debate in international relations remains to be undecided about whether interventions can be purely driven by humanitarian intentions and/or motivations, it appears that over the years many scholars have accepted the fact that humanitarian crises may require a certain incentive for states to intervene. Especially the camp of the realist school recognized that humanitarian intervention is never purely humanitarian in its motivation due to the fact that the main actors are states, which act out of a mix of short-term and long-term interests.[141] Realists state that since the decisions to intervene in humanitarian crises are political decisions made by political decision makers, the motivation to intervene or abstain from intervention will most likely not be completely free from self-interest, prudence and political opportunism.[142] In normative theory it becomes increasingly accepted that humanitarian interventions are mostly based on a mixed ground of motives "[...] where moral considerations, the interests of the people suffering are present as well as national and international interests [...]".[143]

---

[138] Pogge (2006).

[139] Nardin (2006) Op. Cit. 121 (p. 11).

[140] Teson (1988).

[141] Fixdal and Smith (1998) Op. Cit. 82 (p.284).

[142] Roberts (1993) Op. Cit. 19 (p.446).

[143] Ryter (2003) Op. Cit. 17 (p.18).

References

Bose M, Perotti R (2002) From cold war to new world order: the foreign policy of George HW Bush. Greenwood Publishing Group, Westport CT p. 262

Giddens A (1990) The consequences of modernity: self and society in the late modern age. Stanford University Press, Cambridge p. 21

Smith A et al (2001) Introduction in the globalization of world politics—an introduction to international relations. Oxford University Press, Oxford p. 8

Ayoob M (2002) Humanitarian intervention and state sovereignty. int j Human Rights, 6:1, pp. 81–102. Routledge Publisher, London p. 82

Helmke B (2004) OCEANIC—conference on international studies. Conference papers: humanitarian intervention: exemplifying the changing ground rules for the international use of force. ANU College of Asia and the Pacific, Canberra, AU p. 6

Rosenau J (1999) States, sovereignty, and diplomacy in the information age. Paper presented at the ISA conference, virtual diplomacy: a revolution in diplomatic affairs. 18 February 1999. United States Institute of Peace, Washington, DC

Held D et al (1999) Global transformations: Politics, economics, and culture. Stanford University Press, Cambridge p. 49

Domagala A (2004) Humanitarian intervention: the utopia of just war? The NATO intervention in Kosovo and the restraints of humanitarian intervention. The Sussex European Institute Working Papers. University of Sussex, Brighton, UK p. 7

Finnemore M (2003) The purpose of intervention. Cornell University Press, Ithaca, NY p. 9

Kaldor M (1999) New and old wars: organized violence in a global era, 1st edn. Stanford University Press, Cambridge, p. 93

Kishlansky M (2001) Sources of the west: readings in western civilization, 4th edn. Longman, New York, p. 322

McGrew A (2001) Globalization and global politics in the globalization of world politics—an introduction to international relations. (Smith A. & Baylis. J.). Oxford University Press, Oxford p. 25

Oppenheim L (1955) International law. Lauterpacht H (ed) A treatise, Peace. vol 1 London. p. 305

Farer T et al. (2005) Roundtable: humanitarian intervention after 9/11. International relations 19, p. 211 ff Sage Publications on Behalf of the David Davies Memorial Institute for International Studies, London p. 212

Aquinas T (1947) The summa theologica. Benzinger Brothers, New York p. Q94a2

Augustine of Hippo St. (427 (1984)). City of God. Translated by Henry Bettenson Penguin, London p. 862

Bellamy AJ (2004) Motives, outcomes, intent and the legitimacy of humanitarian intervention. J Military Ethics, vol 3:3, Taylor & Francis, London pp. 216–232

Bentham J (1962) Principles of international law. In: Bowring J (ed) The works of Jeremy Bentham. Russell & Russell, New York p. 544

Bjorna C (2009).Legitimising the use of force in international politics: Kosovo, Iraq and the ethics of intervention. Routledge, London p. 48

Boulden B (2001) Peace enforcement: the United Nations experience in Congo, Somalia, and Bosnia. Praeger Publishers, Westport, CT p. 15

Bush GHW (1990) Address before a joint session of congress. The miller center of public affairs. University of Virgina, Charlottesville Retrieved November 5th, 2009 from http://millercenter.org/scripps/archive/speeches/detail/3425 September 11, 1990

Canning J (2003) The political thought of Baldus de Ubaldis. Volume 6 of Cambridge studies in medieval life and thought. Translation from Latin: The king in his kingdom is the emperor of his kingdom. Cambridge University Press Cambridge, UK p. 97

Chesterman S (2003) Just war or just peace? humanitarian intervention and international law. Oxford University Press, Oxford p. 15

Chopra J, Weiss TG (1992) Sovereignty is no longer sacrosanct: codifying humanitarian intervention. Ethics and international affairs Vol 6 Carnegie Council, New York City, NY pp. 95–117

Cicero MT (1928) De Re publica and De legibus. Havard University Press, Cambridge, MA p. 211

UN Security Council (1991) 2982nd Meeting. Resolution 688 (1991). Available: Readex/Index to United Nations Documents and Publication. (S/RES/688). 5 April 1991

UN Security Council (2006) 5430th meeting. Resolution 1674 (2006). Protection of civilians in armed conflict. Available: Readex/Index to United Nations Documents and Publication. (S/RES/1674). 28 April 2006

Dobos N (2008) Justifying humanitarian intervention for the people who pay for it. Praxis, vol 1, No. 1, Spring 2008. Manchester University, Manchester UK p. 42

Donnelly J (1995) State sovereignty and international intervention: the case of human rights. In: Lyons GM and Mastanduno M (eds) Beyond Westphalia? State sovereignty and international intervention Johns Hopkins University Press, Baltimore pp. 115–146

Erasmus D (1917) The complaint of peace. Translated from the Querela Pacis by Thomas Paynell (A.D. 1521) of Erasmus. Open Court, Chicago p. 82

Evans G, Sahnoun M (2002) The responsibility to protect. Foreign affairs, Vol. 81 No. 6 (Nov—Dec 2002). Council on Foreign Relations, New York, pp. 99–110

Fixdal M, Smith D (1998) Humanitarian intervention and just war. Mershon international studies review, Vol 42, No. 2 Blackwell Publishing on behalf of the international studies association, Hoboken, NJ pp. 283–312

Garrett J (2004) Just war theory based on human rights. Bowling Green: Western Kentucky University. Retrieved November 14th, 2009 from http://web2.wku.edu/~jan.garrett/ethics/jwtbhrts.htm Revised 28 Oct 2004

Goodin RE (1995) Utilitarianism as a public philosophy. Cambridge University Press, Cambridge, UK p. 18

Greenwood C (1993) Is there a right of humanitarian intervention? The World Today Vol 49 Chatham House, London pp. 34–40

Grotius H (2001) De Jure Belli ac Pacis. Translated by A.C. Campbell. Kitchener, Batoche Books, Ontario (Book II, Ch. XXV, § VIII, p. 247)

Grünfeld F (2007) The failure to prevent genocide in Rwanda; the role of Bystanders. Brill, Leiden p. 216

Hieronymi O (1996) The Evasion of State Responsibility and the Lessons from Rwanda: the need for a new concept of collective security. J Refugee Studies vol 9(3) Oxford University Press, Oxford, pp. 236–239

Holzgrefe JL, Keohane RO (2003) Humanitarian intervention: ethical, legal and political dilemmas. Cambridge University Press, Cambridge, UK p. 19

ICISS (2001) The responsibility to protect. The report of the international commission on intervention and state sovereignty. International Development Research Center, Ottawa p. IX

Johnson JT (1984) Can modern war be just? Yale University Press, New Haven, CT p. 11

Knudsen TB (2009) The history of humanitarian intervention—the rule or the exception? Paper presented at the annual meeting of the ISA's 50th annual convention exploring the past, anticipating the future, New York Marriott Marquis, New York City, NY. p. 5

Kurt Tucholsky cited by Nicolaus F (2003) Kriegspropaganda, P.M. Magazin April 2003. p. 94

Lawrence TJ (1925) The principles of international law, Seventh Edition by Percy H.Winfield, Macmillan, London pp. 127–128

Leifer M (1993) Vietnam's intervention in kampuchea: the rights of state versus the rights of people. In: Forbes I and Hoffman M (eds) Political theory, international relations, and the ethics of intervention. St. Martin's Press, Basingstoke p. 146 ff

McCarthey L (1993) International anarchy, realism, and non-intervention. In: Forbes I and Hoffman M (eds) Political theory, inter-national relations and the ethics of intervention, St. Martin's Press, Basingstoke pp. 75–90

McQueen C (2006) Humanitarian intervention and safety zones: Iraq, Bosnia and Rwanda. London: Palgrave. p. 13
Mednicoff DM (2006) Humane wars? International law, just war theory and contemporary armed humanitarian intervention. Law, culture and the humanities, vol 2 Sage Publications, London p. 379
Nardin T (2006) Introduction. In: Nardin, Terry and Williams, Vanessa (eds) Humanitarian intervention. New York University Press, New York p. 10
Ottaway M, Lacina B (2003) International interventions and imperialism: lessons from the 1990s. SAIS Review vol. XXIII no. 2 (Summer–Fall 2003). John Hopkins University Press, Washington D.C, p. 76
Parekh B (1997) Rethinking humanitarian intervention. International political science review, Vol 18(1) Sage Publications, London pp. 55–74
Pastor R (1993) Forward to the beginning: widening the scope for global collective action. Int J Vol 48 Canadian International Council, Toronto pp. 641–667
Pogge T (2006) Moralizing humanitarian intervention: why jurying fails and how law can work. In: Nardin T and Williams V (eds) Humanitarian intervention. New York University Press, New York p. 166
Ramsbotham O, Woodhouse T (1996) Humanitarian intervention in contemporary conflict. Polity, Cambridge, UK pp. 14–18
Ramsey P (1986) War and the christian conscience: how shall modern war be conducted justly? Duke University Press, Durham, NC p. 40
Reisman M (1985) Criteria for the lawful use of force in international law. Yale J Int Law, vol 10. Yale University Press, New Haven, CT
Reisman MW (1990) Sovereignty and human rights in contemporary international law. Am J Int Law Vol 84. The American Society of International Law, Washington, D.C pp. 866–876
Roberts A (1993) Humanitarian war: military intervention and human rights. International affairs (Royal Institute of International Affairs 1944-), vol 69, No. 3, Blackwell Publishing, London, pp. 429–449
Rodley NS (1992) Collective intervention to protect human rights. In: Rodley NS (ed) To loosen the bands of wickedness. Brassey's, London: p. 37
Ryter MA (2003) Motives for humanitarian intervention and the international community. Helsinki: National Defence College/Maanpuolustuskorkeakoulu. p. 5
Scharf M (1998) Results of the Rome conference for an international criminal court. ASIL Insights, August 1998. Washington, D.C.: The American society of international law. retrieved 9th Nov 2009 from http://www.asil.org/insigh23.cfm
Seay M (2007) Realism, liberlism and humanitarian intervention: Is there a middle ground? Independent academic research studies, paper on human rights and equality. IARS, London p. 5 Retrieved September 13th, 2009 from http://www.iars.org.uk/HR%20papers.htm
Shaw MN (1995) International law. 3rd edn. Cambridge University Press, Cambridge UK p. 684
Skinner Q (1978) The foundations of modern political thought. Cambridge University Press, Cambridge, UK p. 244
Smith MJ (1998) Humanitarian intervention: an overview of the ethical issues. Ethics and International Affairs Journal 12(1):Carnegie Council, New York City, NY pp. 63–79
Solomon N (2005) Judaism and the ethics of war. International review of the Red Cross, vol 87, No. 858 Cambridge University Press, Cambridge, UK p. 298
Stowell EC (1921) Intervention in international law. John Byrne & Co, Washington DC pp. 515–516
Taylor P, Curtis D (2007) The United nation in the globalization of world politics—an introduction to international relations. (Smith A. and Baylis. J.). Oxford University Press, Oxford p. 322
Teson FR (1988) Humanitarian intervention: an inquiry into law and morality. Transnational Publishers, Dobbs Ferry, N.Y p. 106–107
Teson FR (2005) Ending tyranny in Iraq. Ethics and international affairs. vol 19, No. 2, Carnegie Council, New York City, NY pp. 1–20

The International Court of Justice (1951) Advisory opinion in the matter of reservations to the convention on the prevention and punishment of the crime of genocide. 18th May 1951. Retrieved December 12th 2010 from http://www.icj-cij.org/docket/files/12/4283.pdf
The United Nations Secretary General (1992) Report of the secretary-general pursuant to the statement adopted by the summit meeting of the security council on 31 January 1992: an agenda for peace preventive diplomacy, peacemaking and peace-keeping. Available: Readex/ Index to United Nations documents and publication. 17 June 1992. (A/47/277–S/24111). p. 2
UN Department for peacekeeping operations. What is peacekeeping? Retrieved October 22nd, 2009 from http://www.un.org/Depts/dpko/dpko/field/body_pkeep.htm
United Nations (1945) Charter of the United Nations. 24 October 1945, 1 UNTS XVI. Preamble. p. 1
United Nations General Assembly (1948) Resolution 260 III A. Convention on the prevention and punishment of the crime of genocide. January 12th 1951. United Nations Treaty Series (U.N.T.S) No. 1021, vol. 78 (1951), p. 277. Art. IV
United Nations General Assembly (1965). 1408th plenary session. Declaration on the inadmissibility of intervention in the domestic affairs of states. Available: index to United Nations documents and publications. (UNGA Res. 2131/XX)
United Nations General Assembly (1998) Rome statute of the international criminal court (last amended January 2002), Available: Readex/Index to United Nations documents and publication. 17 July 1998. (A/CONF. 183/9) (Art. 25 [2])
UN General Assembly (2005) 60th session. Draft resolution 60/L1. Follow-up to the outcome of the millennium summit: 2005 world summit outcome. Available: Index to United Nations documents and publications. (A/60/L.1). 15 December 2005 p. 31
United Nations Secretariat (2004) Secretariat general's high-level panel on threats, challenges and change. A more secure world: our shared responsibility. United Nations department of public information, New York p. 48
Vincent RJ (1974) Non-Intervention and international order. Princeton University Press, Princeton, NJ p. 13
Verwey W (1992) The legality of humanitarian intervention after the cold war. In: Ferris E (ed) A challenge to intervene: a new role for the United Nations? Life and Peace Institute, Uppsala, SE p. 114
Verwey W cited in Malanczuk P (1993) Humanitarian intervention and the legitimacy of the use of force. Uitgeverij Het Spinhuis, Amsterdam p. 40
Walzer M (2006) Just and unjust wars. Basic Books, New York p. 107
Weiss TG (2007) Humanitarian intervention: ideas in action. Polity Press, Malden, MA p. 63
Welin AF (2005) Minimal solidarism: post-cold war responses to humanitarian crisis. Linköping Universitet. MSc in International and European Relations. Master's Thesis, August 2005. LIU-EKI/INT–05/022—SE. Linkoping, SE: Linkoping University. p. 2
Wheeler N (2002) Saving strangers: humanitarian intervention in international society. Oxford University Press, Oxford p. 141
Wheeler N and Bellamy A (2008) Humanitarian intervention in world politics. In: Baylis J and Smith S (eds) The globalization of world politics: an introduction to international relations, Oxford University Press, Oxford p. 525

Chapter 2
National Interests and Altruism in Humanitarian Intervention

In the following chapter I will discuss in detail how realist and cosmopolitan theories approach the motivation for humanitarian intervention. The first sub-chapter will clarify why and to what extend realism assigns considerable importance to national/self-interests in the decision making process surrounding the question of whether to intervene in a humanitarian crisis or not. The second sub-chapter will make an argument for the prevalence of altruism as the primary motivation for humanitarian intervention from a moralist point of view. This chapter will facilitate the understanding of the qualitative research presented in the subsequent chapter where the motivation for post-1990 humanitarian interventions will be presented.

2.1 Humanitarian Intervention and National Interest

2.1.1 Definition of National Interest/Self-Interest

The term 'humanitarian' describing an intervention aimed at providing relief for individuals in danger grants the concept of humanitarian intervention a rather charitable, philanthropic or even altruistic connotation. However, this connotation stands in stark contrast to one widely accepted assumption deriving from realism that states in the international arena should and do base their actions on self-interest or in a broader sense national interests.[1] National interests are subject to redefinition by the policy makers and need to be defined before they can be defended. "[...] The meaning of national interest can vary widely, from increasing a state's power to a survival of a state to upholding international legitimacy [...]".[2] Commonly, based on the realist notion, national interests are narrowly defined as the sum of material and security interest of a nation.

[1] Richardson (1997). (p. 1).
[2] Acharya (2003). (p. 2).

A. Krieg, *Motivations for Humanitarian Intervention*, SpringerBriefs in Ethics,
DOI: 10.1007/978-94-007-5374-7_2, © The Author(s) 2013

Due to the fact that the concept of humanitarian intervention has evolved from the ethical debate about making resources available for helping others, national interests would appear to have no place as a motivation for humanitarian intervention. In particular, moralists tend to have a very low opinion of national interests, as the concept is generally based on the assumption that national interests are equal to self-interest or selfishness. Mistakenly, perhaps, self-interest and selfishness are conceived to be intertwined, causing self-interest to be often identified as self-absorption, egoism, and the disregard for the rights and interests of others.[3] The negative connotation arising from the definition of self-interest in economics is adopted by political science as a motivation based on "[...] money making, avarice and greed, materialism, hedonism, the profit motive or profit maximization [...]".[4] The notion of the *homo economicus* in the philosophy of Adam Smith, however, may be appreciated since the human face of self-interest is understood as advancing the interest of all by pursuing one's own self-interest.[5] This idea only holds if one steps away from the definition of self-interest as selfishness. In fact, the pursuance of self-interest or national interests for that matter is only selfish and blameworthy if it disregards the interests of others where their interests ought not to be ignored. As long as individuals or states follow their rational drive of satisfying one's own needs first, society can work efficiently as resources are allocated efficiently.[6]

This assumption is echoed by scholars of the realist school such as Morgenthau, who introduced this notion to international relations theory. Morgenthau argued that "[...] if states pursue only their rational self-interests, without defining them too grandly, they will collide with other states only minimally [...]",[7] i.e. as long as states follow their own narrow interests the world can be a peaceful place. Morgenthau's definition of national interests derives from Machiavelli's 15th century pessimistic realism, where the interests of the state are characterized as the self-absorbed definition of the interests of the state and its community. Thereby, this definition is distinctly different from earlier medieval beliefs that gave precedence to a more universal definition of the interests of the state based on moral Christian values. In a world characterized by anarchy and the Hobbesian notion of "[...] homo homini lupus [...]"[8] states are allowed to take all means to protect themselves and to ensure their survival. As Morgenthau defines national interests in terms of power, the sovereign as a servant of his society is trusted with the role to preserve or even improve the state's power *vis-à-vis* other states. Nonetheless, not all national interests can be categorized as equally important. Morgenthau distinguishes between vital and secondary national interests. To preserve the former,

3 Maitland (2002). (p. 4).

4 Ibid.

5 Ibid.

6 Ibid (p. 5).

7 Roskin (1994). (p. 2).

8 Lat. Transation = *man is man's wolf* in Hobbes (1990). (p. 87).

which directly concern the essential survival of the state, Morgenthau does not compromise any option short of the use of force. Hence, vital national interest can be relatively easily defined as being concerned with the state as a free and independent nation as well as with the protection of institutions, people and fundamental rights. Morgenthau defines secondary national interests as those removed from the state's borders not threatening the security or integrity of the nation. Therefore, these peripheral interests can be compromised in case the expected benefits are outweighed by anticipated costs.[9]

In contemporary studies national interests are oftentimes divided into subcategories along a scale indicating the urgency of the national interests at stake. Very high urgency interests are those interests connected to the survival of the nation while vital national interests indicate only a high urgency. Moderate and low urgency interests correspond to major and peripheral interests respectively. Survival interests have a very high urgency and therefore may trigger states to mobilize all national resources to defend them. Vital interests are critical and involve the defence of close allies or strategic resources. Major national interests are less critical and only represent a moderate level of urgency since they are concerned with the protection of less important allies and non-critical resources. From a realist point of view, the degree of urgency of national interests at stake determines the extent of the effort a state is allowed to invest in defending these interests. Consequently, the higher the urgency of the interests at stake, the more costs in terms of troops, time, money, equipment, resources, political prestige or economic aid the state is willing to devote to the defence of these interests.[10] Whereas survival and vital interests necessitate the use of force, realists do not deem the use of force compulsory when defending major national interests. As low urgency peripheral national interests do not involve the protection of the nation's heartland and do not pose an immediate physical security threat to the nation, the defence of such peripheral interests may only involve humanitarian or reconstruction efforts, not however, the deployment of large numbers of combat troops.[11]

Apart from this narrow realist definition, national interests can also be defined in a broader sense as advancing more universal interests concerned with the wellbeing of mankind. Realists, though, find a dichotomy between national interest and values, disregarding the fact that the desire to assist the less fortunate is an enduring feature and underlying value of Western political culture.[12] Based on the claim that it is in the self-interest of every state to preserve global stability and care for global humanity, states may define their national interests in terms of liberal Western values such as democracy, liberalism or human rights.[13] Western states

[9] Morgenthau (1985). (p. 5).

[10] Keifer (2003). (p. 6).

[11] Slenska (2007). (p. 4).

[12] Shibata (2006). (p. 27).

[13] Walzer (1995). Op. Cit. 1 (p. 54).

assign great importance to the preservation of the legacy of Western culture and its values rooted in Graeco-Roman classical culture, the Judaeo-Christian heritage and the post-Enlightenment philosophy.[14] Though serving an ethical purpose, promoting these values beyond national borders might nonetheless serve the national self-interest. In particular American national interests are often defined as a hybrid of security related interests in the realist sense and of value-related interests comprising the intrinsic ethic and moral values that have been laid down in the U.S. Constitution. The US republic's *raison d'etat*, which in an extended way is understood to be constructed based on universal values, regards the preservation of global humanity and the proliferation of liberal human values a vital national interests.[15] Thus, despite taking into account the moral value-related aspects of national interests, the preservation and promotion of these Western values remains a self-interested undertaking. Because exporting Western values such as democracy, human rights or the liberal market economy does ultimately serve the interests of the West due to the fact that countries based on similar values are more likely to become lucrative trading partners or political allies.

In this study national interests are narrowly defined as the self-interest of a state or nation. As to be able to make a clear distinction between national interests and self-interest, the former is defined narrowly without any considerations of possible moral connotations. National/self-interest in this study will be described as a composition of narrow national interests, i.e. economic and strategic interests, and the personal political interests of the political decision makers. That is to say, acting according to national interests includes actions based on economic interests and strategic interests, as well as the interests of personal political or material gains of policy makers. Thereby, intervention motivated by the aim to seize vital mineral resources is in the same way driven by national interests as an intervention that is motivated by the policy maker's desire to advance his political interests during election times.

2.1.2 National Interest and Social Contractarianism

A strong argument for the prevalence of national interests as the prime motivation for state action including humanitarian intervention comes from realist social contractarianism. Realist social contractarianism rejects the moralist argument that humanitarian intervention must be purely humanitarian in its intend, i.e. the protection of the freedom, rights and interests of people in another state. Allen Buchanan argues that the international legitimacy of humanitarian intervention has to take precedence over the external legitimacy. That is to say, governments do not

[14] See Spielvogel (2004).

[15] William (2005). (p. 318)

only have to justify the intervention externally as humanitarian, but also internally to its own citizens as an efficient intervention in terms of a cost-benefit analysis.

The approach presented in this book so far established the external legitimacy or illegitimacy of humanitarian intervention, namely whether humanitarian intervention can be justified to the people living outside the intervening state, to the international community or its intended beneficiaries. The ethical debate, however, rarely seems to elaborate on the internal legitimacy of humanitarian intervention, i.e. if it can be justified to the taxpayers who have to pay for it or the soldiers who are sent to risk their lives in the crisis region. According to both Hobbes and Locke, the state's *raison d'être* is to ensure the security and wellbeing of the people that bring the state into existence through the social contract. That is to say, that the social contract is a construct by a certain group of people, named a discretionary association, with the primary purpose to protect these individuals from the perils and 'inconveniences' of the state of nature. Every individual in a state submits to the authority of the state in order to receive in return protection and security.[16]

> [...] On this view, citizens empower their government to act as an agent or trustee for the sole purpose of promoting their interests. They [...] relinquish a portion of their earnings in tax in return for this service [...].[17]

The state is to be understood as the benefactor for its own citizens acting exclusively in their interests due to the fact that

> [...] No one else's interests are represented, so legitimate political authority is naturally defined as authority exercised for the good of the parties to the contract, the citizens of this state [...].[18]

According to Buchanan the state itself receives its legitimacy primarily from the service it renders to its citizens; hence, benefaction is what gives the state the right to rule. Quite to the contrary, states or governments do not have the obligation to serve the world at large. Further, according to realist social contractarians, the government does not have any inherent legitimacy in itself but is a sole agent of the discretionary association it represents. Therefore, for governments to engage both internally and externally to practises that do not serve the primary interest of its citizens would be morally wrong. Charles Krauthammer continues by stating that since statesmen or governments are no more than people's trustees spending the blood and treasure of others, their freedom to wage war or intervene militarily is limited to cases where it is strategically necessary or where it renders an increase in domestic benefits. Therefore, if intervention occurs in order to secure natural resources or sea ways that are of particular national interests to the intervening state, intervention is acceptable. If on the contrary invention occurs for

16 Dobos (2009). (p. 3).

17 Dobos (2008). Op. Cit. 123 (p. 35).

18 Buchanan (1999). (p. 75).

the sole purpose of pleasing international law, world public opinion or public sentiments of crucial allies, intervention is not internally justifiable.[19]

It follows that purely humanitarian intervention as envisaged by moralists and altruists is commonly rejected by realist social contractarianists for the simple reason that intervening governments invest both the lives and funds of their own people in order to save strangers who are not part of the social contract. Thereby, foreigners become beneficiaries of funds and soldiers lives that have been transferred to the state in the belief that the state will use them in the best possible manner to advance national interests and thereby the social well-being of all citizens of the state. It is believed that a state that invests in intervention for humanitarian purposes compromises the security of its own citizens in the process due to the fact that a state cannot defend strangers abroad and then still retain the funds necessary to pay for the protection of its citizens at home.[20] Thus, a state engaging in a purely humanitarian intervention violates its fiduciary obligation: to act in the best interests of the nation. If resources are directed towards a disinterested intervention these allocations are considered to be dead investments as they do not render any material returns. If intervention occurs for self-interested motives, resources are allocated to a venture that has at least the prospect of rendering material gains. Buchanan argues that even if the majority of citizens would be altruistic enough to allocate their resources to an intervention for purely humanitarian purposes, intervention would not be justified as the state would invest the funds of others that oppose this intervention.[21] Apart from the financial resources employed in a military intervention, it remains even more questionable if the state has the right to deploy soldiers, conscripted as well as professionals, to defend the human rights of strangers. Soldiers enter the military with the readiness to risk their lives for the defence of the community only. In fact the implicit moral contract between the state and its armed forces

> […] obliges military personnel to run grave risks and to engage in morally and personally difficult actions. They do these things on the basis of the implicit promise that the circumstances under which they must act are grounded in political leadership's good faith judgment that the defense of sovereignty and integrity of the nation (or, by careful extension, the nation's vital interests) […].[22]

Consequently, any armed intervention to preserve the interests of others, i.e. not national interests, but still jeopardizing the lives of the soldiers would be morally wrong. Trying to prevent or avert the loss of lives of individuals abroad by jeopardizing the lives of one's own citizens would not be ethically defendable, since according to the social contract every state should first of all care for the well-being and lives of its own citizens.

---

19 Krauthammer (1985). (p. 11).

20 Dobos (2008). Op. Cit. 123 (p. 39).

21 Buchanan (1999) Op. Cit. 162 (p. 76).

22 Cook (2000). (p. 62).

Critiques of the realist social contract theory argue, however, that not only the citizens have a contract with the state but also that the state has a contract through international legal instruments with the international community at large. International law binds the state to universal international norms, which dictate the defence of human rights beyond national borders.[23] However, as international law does not impose a perfect duty on the state to intervene for humanitarian purposes, the state itself is in fact not bound by any second contract that might take precedence over the social contract. For this, the international community would need the establishment of a credible and enforceable human rights regime that does not only authorize but actually impose the duty on all states to intervene in cases of supreme humanitarian emergency. Only then, the social contract between the citizens and their state would become a subsidiary to an international contract between states to form a community that fosters the duty of humanitarian intervention. Only then, intervention for purely humanitarian interests would actually become a national interest and had to be pursued by states disregarding the willingness of their citizens to allocate resources and lives.

2.1.3 The Role of Self-Interest in Humanitarian Intervention

Based on the realist discretionary association argument, realism strongly opposes the use of a state's financial and military resources for advancing anything other than the interests of the state's citizens. Due to the fact that realism is grounded on the pessimistic world view of an international system that is characterized by actors trying to maximize their utility at the expense of others, realists find themselves in a constant perpetual security dilemma. Therefore, each state has to try to maximize its own power in relation to other players in the arena while providing primarily for the security and welfare of its own people. Committing to military activities beyond this *raison d'etat* such as helping strangers, can therefore never be justified since purely humanitarian intervention does not help to maximize a state's own power.[24] Hence, a just intervention in the realist world has to be based on a motivation according to the state's interests.

While some realists would rule out any intervention on humanitarian grounds as not to confuse foreign policy with philanthropy, others might accept intervention in order to help those in need so long as it does not challenge any core security interests of the state or impose high costs in terms of financial resources or loss of life.[25] Therefore, some realists argue that humanitarian intervention has occurred, for example in the 1990s, as a particular foreign policy tool in international relations

[23] Dobos (2009). Op. Cit. 160 (p. 5).

[24] Bellamy (2003). (p. 10).

[25] Wheeler (2004).(p. 6).

> [...] in situations where it is relatively cheap, is against a militarily weak nation, operates in a location that is accessible and strategically important, where public opinion is in favour and the intervention does not interfere with other political and economic objectives [...].[26]

That is to say, due to the fact that states realize that humanitarian interventions are real military operations connected to real costs, states do only what is necessary to uphold their reputation without actually focusing on what has to be done. The reason is that the benefits of humanitarian interventions are unclear or are arguably distributed mostly among free-loaders, whereas the substantial costs of intervention, as in every military operation, have to be borne by the intervening party. Therefore, leaders, in particular of democratic states, will have to invest a lot of efforts in carefully framing the costs of intervention, and the benefits as well as the probability of success in order to generate public support for the decisions taken.[27] It follows that if a certain humanitarian crisis does not affect national interests, statesmen are confronted with a dilemma of keeping costs low in order to receive internal legitimization while in the same time following an international call for intervention in order to receive external legitimization.

Some realists conclude that

> [...] interventions motivated by general moral justifications or conceptual appeals to the validity of international order will either fail to occur or will succumb to half-hearted commitments (as the cases of Rwanda and Somalia showed [...].[28]

Hence, according to this statement governments only tolerate the losses and costs of intervention that actually serve the national interest. The fewer the national interests involved, the more governments are inclined to either remain passive or keep the costs minimal. Realists bring forward examples of interventions such as Operation Restore Hope in Somalia 1993 to back up their claims, to show that the US public backed up the operation only as long as feeding the starving population did not cost any lives. When eighteen soldiers were killed in a single day the operation had to be terminated as public opinion threatened to harm the governments' political standing. Krauthammer argues that therefore humanitarian intervention has no future, for the simple reason that it involves the contradicting concept of bloodless war.[29] The adoption of a risk-averse strategy brings about, if at all, ineffective interventions by soldiers whose right to use force is constrained by Rules of Engagement to such an extent that the military assets deployed cannot unleash their full potential.[30] Western governments are in

---

[26] Chinkin (2000). (p. 37).

[27] Boettcher (2004). (p. 333).

[28] Wesley (2005). (p. 58).

[29] Krauthammer (1999). (p. 3).

[30] Casualty averse strategies relying solely on air power without any substantial ground support constrained by altitude margins do not only cause considerable collateral damage but also make the achievement of military objectives highly ineffective. Due to changing realties in the combat theatre caused by irregular tactics and strategies employed by insurgent groups, far distance or

particular attracted to air power against technologically less advanced opponents as it allows air crews to operate under the minimal risk of being shot down. Both forms of intervention, restricted use of ground forces or the sole reliance on of air power, minimize costs at least in terms of lives for the intervener but might in fact increase the loss of lives on the side of the civilian beneficiaries. In the case of Kosovo 1999 Western interveners chose certain military strategies with the purpose of increasing the safety of their own soldiers, while in the same time making the means of warfare disproportionate since force was employed indiscriminately. In Kosovo"[...] casualty-free intervention was achieved at the expense of inflicting great suffering on [...] civilians [...]".[31]

In order to make humanitarian interventions more effective, realists argue that national interests must prevail in the decision to intervene. The higher the expected utility, i.e. the interest for the nation and the decision-maker, the higher the risks the decision maker is willing to take in order to achieve his objectives. If the interests in a humanitarian crisis are only peripheral, intervention will only occur in a limited nature, if at all. Therefore, self-interested motivations have to be an inherent part of humanitarian intervention. Indeed, national interests cannot be divorced from humanitarianism or altruism as according to realists, governments are rational egoists who act in their pursuit of their interests. Raising national interests during humanitarian intervention is a prerequisite for an intervention on basis of otherwise humanitarian grounds.[32]

Apart from merely stating that national interests should prevail in the decision to intervene, some realist go even that far as to state that states would never intervene unless vital national interests are at stake, a claim entirely negating the existence of altruism in international relations. Wheeler (2000) states that realism in its purest form is based on the contention that "[...] states will not intervene for primarily humanitarian reasons because they are always motivated by considerations of national self-interest [...]".[33] According to this assumption states are rational actors that are not guided by emotional considerations; the fact that decisions makers, however, might be emotional in their decision-making is completely disregarded. Thus, conservative realism would argue that the results of the research conducted in this book will demonstrate that altruism has never been a

(Footnote 30 continued)
high altitude munitions have oftentimes difficulties to accurately eliminate targets. The reason is that insurgency warfare relies on highly mobile forces that can operate in disguise among the civilian population, which make it difficult for spotters and air men alike to engage a target from far distance without having the ability to identify the targets validity and exact position. Relying on far distance and high altitude munitions can cause highly disproportionate damage to civilians and civilian infrastructure without effectively eliminating valid military targets. [See Cooper (2001). (p. 85)].

[31] Atack (2002). (p. 289).

[32] Farer et al. (2005) Op. Cit 24 (p. 228).

[33] Wheeler (2000). (p. 30).

primary motivator for humanitarian intervention, but only a minor motivation secondary to national interest maximization.

2.1.4 National Interests and the Fear of the Trojan Horse

The importance of national interests in current foreign affairs has stoked the concerns in some circles that the concept of humanitarian intervention is no more than a means of powerful Western countries to broaden their influence and guarantee their access to vital resources. The fear of what scholars name neo-colonialism has been intensified by the recent experience of the usage of humanitarian rhetoric to justify the interventions in Afghanistan 2001 and Iraq 2003. "[…] Fear of a new imperialism is particularly acute in parts of the world that have known colonization, where international interventions revive memories of the imperial past […]".[34]

Due to the fact that Western governments have promoted Western values of liberalism and democracy abroad and in the post-Cold War era have used their economic, political and military superiority to correct humanitarian grievances abroad, many in the non-Western world have come to regard the concept of coercive intervention for humanitarian purposes quite sceptically. Unlike pure peace-keeping missions that require the consent of the receiving country and lack any coercive nature, the emerging humanitarian intervention regime enables Western states to take all measures necessary to bring humanitarian crises to a halt with or without the consent of the receiving state.[35] Despite the fact that outside interventions in the last two decades have become less exploitative and abusive in comparison to 19th century imperialism, many international interventions in the post-Cold War era have nonetheless aimed at regime change and/or nation-building along Western liberal lines. While some instances such as Operation Uphold Democracy in Haiti 1994 were designed to re-install a democratically elected regime, post-conflict resolutions such as in Afghanistan or Iraq have relied on the installation of local transitional governments usually closely affiliated to the intervening parties. In the cases of Kosovo or East-Timor, the international community has even taken over the role of the administrator itself by setting up an international administration.[36] Together with the creation of a political elite, Western states further support the new regimes by training security as well as administrative personnel. Thus, it seems plausible that the intervention of foreign governments into the internal affairs of another country has a tremendous impact on the sovereignty and autonomy of the receiving state. Even though the reshaping of state affairs usually occurs under the pretext of humanitarian support, the

---

[34] Ottaway and Lacina (2003). Op. Cit. 56 (p. 74).

[35] Ibid (p. 76).

[36] Ibid (p. 83).

adherence to national interests by Western governments creates the fear that the toleration of humanitarian intervention by most powerful states allows for a legal remodelling of state structure by foreign interveners.

> [...] Given the disparity in power among states, humanitarian intervention has the strong potential of becoming a tool for the interference by the strong into the affairs of the weak, with humanitarian considerations providing a veneer to justify such intervention [...].[37]

States that present a weak human rights record and are militarily inferior to the main Western powers reject the concept of humanitarian intervention out of a fear that a humanitarian rationale could be used against them to undermine their sovereignty. In particular Muslim states are under increasing pressure by Western governments as several countries could easily be targeted in the war against terror for strategic interests as well as for humanitarian considerations due to their weak human rights record. After decades of political struggle against and emancipation from Western influence in the 20th century, the West's former colonies are confronted with a reality where the responsibility to protect and other soft laws passed by the UN, have created a situation where intervention becomes practically possible also for the interests of the great powers. The concern that humanitarian interventions are "[...] noble in name but potentially spurious in intent [...]"[38] was further intensified by the interventions in the post 9/11 era where the Bush Doctrine allowed for unilateral preventive intervention in case of non-immanent threat. Operation Enduring Freedom and particularly Operation Iraqi Freedom have possibly undermined the credibility of the West as a humanitarian and altruistic actor in the Muslim world. The Bush Doctrine is believed to have given the United States the right in a unipolar world to intervene in the name of common humanity.[39] Condemning the allied operation in Iraq as a form of neo-colonialism Syrian President Assad stated that he considered Syria to be the next target on the list.[40] In the UN debate surrounding the possibility of intervening in Darfur in 2004 the Arab government of Sudan objected to intervention from outsiders, refusing to see the humanitarian aspect of such an operation. Instead, the ambassador of Sudan to the UN made a statement during a Security Council meeting clearly affirming the fear that intervention might come to serve the interests of the intervening Western parties. The ambassador wondered

> [...] if the Sudan would have been safe from the hammer of the Security Council even if there had been no crisis in Darfur, and whether the Darfur humanitarian crisis might not be a Trojan horse? Has this lofty humanitarian objective been adopted and embraced by other people who are advocating a hidden agenda?[41]

---

37 Ayoob (2002). Op. Cit. 8 (p. 92).

38 Nafie (2000). (p. 1).

39 Sid-Ahmed (2000). (p. 3).

40 Wimelius (2009). (p. 16).

41 Bellamy (2009). (p. 113).

The indictment of Sudanese President Al Bashir by the ICC holding him responsible for the genocide in Darfur, was conceived with a similarly negative attitude by Sudanese government officials. The genocide charge was merely understood as a political act, trying to 'obstruct' political affairs in Khartoum.[42]

Thus, it appears as if a combination of the historical legacy of colonialism and the recent experience of ostensible humanitarian interventions have created the fear in former colonies that the West employs the humanitarian argument as a vehicle to bypass the sovereignty principle in order to exploit a countries' wealth in a form of neo-colonialism.

2.2 Humanitarian Intervention and Altruism

2.2.1 Definition of Altruism

Altruism, describing a selfless and other-oriented behaviour, has a difficult standing in international relations as it does in social sciences in general. Describing the complete opposite of self-interest, altruism will be introduced in this book as a motivation entirely detached from the rational and realist notions presented before. The idea that states and political decision makers invest into ventures that will neither benefit themselves personally or the nation at large might seem to be idealistic. Nonetheless, the concept of altruism found its way into international relations, particularly since humanitarian intervention has emerged as an act with the primary purpose of helping others.

The Oxford Dictionary defines altruism as an "[...] unselfish concern for others [...]",[43] thereby making both the intention and the motivation of the action other-oriented. In Zoology altruism refers to the behaviour of an animal that benefits another animals at its own expense. Thus, in this respect altruism refers to an action that is not only not self-enriching but actually self-harming while benefiting someone else. Etymologically, the word altruism derives from the Latin expression *alteri huic*, meaning 'to this other', which was merged in Italian into *altrui*, 'somebody else'.[44] According to Bar Tal (1986) altruism has to satisfy five criteria:

> [...]altruistic behaviour (a) must benefit another person, (b) must be performed voluntarily, (c) must be performed intentionally, (d) the benefit must be the goal by itself, and (e) must be performed without expecting any external reward [...].[45]

---

42 Al Jazeera. Net (2010).

43 Soanes and Stevenson (2005).

44 Ibid.

45 Bar Tal (1986). (p. 5).

Hence, Bar Tal approaches the concept of altruism from the motivation's perspective, describing altruism's inherent value as based on a clear other-oriented, self-less motivation.

For a long time social sciences, economics and even biology regarded altruism as an unrealistic concept not existing in its purest form due to the fact that it was believed that any action taken by an individual or state is always connected to a self-interested motivation. Only in recent years have scholars begun to agree that altruism is an inherent part of human nature and self-preservation, as individuals do contribute to public goods from which they might benefit little or which benefit only their offspring. One of the most prominent advocators of self-interested action and the prevalence of rationality, Adam Smith, stated himself already in the 18th century that

> [...]How selfish soever man be supposed, there are evidently some principles in his nature, which interest him in the fortune of others, and render their happiness necessary to him, though he derives nothing from it, except the pleasure of seeing it [...].[46]

The propensity to help others, even when suffering high costs, without receiving any benefits is a natural behaviour that can be observed among a wide range of different mostly highly socialized species in nature: birds give predator alarms, mother rats endure severe shock to save their infants, baboons help defend their troops and porpoises sustain their injured fellows.[47] Human beings in particular have obtained a strong pro-social behaviour through socialization and the development of norms facilitating social cohabitation. It appears natural to the human species to engage in cooperative social endeavours that benefit others or the community at large, even at a cost to themselves.

Despite the fact that human beings have naturally an inclination to help others and engage in altruistic behaviour, the actual willingness and propensity to do so depends according to Schwartz and Howard (1984) on the peculiarity of the individual personality and the situational context in which the action is undertaken. Generally one can state that individuals that have high self-esteem and are not in need of constant approval as well as are high in moral development are more likely to show altruistic behaviour. Nonetheless, self-less behaviour benefiting others is also strongly triggered by the social norms or socially constructed personal norms that pressure the individual, namely feelings of moral obligation to perform or refrain from certain actions.[48] The same is true for states or political decision makers since the acceptance of humanitarian norms in the international community raises the awareness that helping others in specific situations is at least morally mandatory. Another factor affecting the propensity to help or assist, playing a particular role in state behaviour, is the perception of costs of action. Research has shown that individuals and groups that perceived helping situations

---

46 Smith (1969). (p. 47).

47 Piliavin and Charng (1990). (p. 45).

48 Schwartz and Howard (1984). (p. 234).

as more rewarding and less costly were more inclined to be altruistic. Especially individuals who are less safety-oriented (high in need for security) than esteem-oriented (high in self-efficacy, self-worth), are more likely to help others.[49]

Since even the most altruistic personalities do have limits in their ability to do good for the benefit of others without creating harm to themselves, altruistic action is naturally subject to selectivity. Due to the fact that altruism does not produce any rewards, the action takers are naturally more risk-averse than action takers that act out of self-interested motivations. Action takers that expect a return in any form will most likely invest more assets and are more likely to accept a degree of risk to attain these returns. On the contrary, altruists who by definition cannot accept any rewards for their action will try to avoid risk or at least minimize risk as much as possible. In a world where the propensity to help others first is unequally distributed among individuals, altruistic individuals face a reality where egoists not engaging in self-less behaviour seem to have a clear advantage. Therefore, "[...] the central characteristic of all forms of altruism is this: discrimination is a necessary part of a persisting altruism [...]".[50] In a world where altruism is not an absolute virtue, altruists run the risk of losing ground to egoists that approach life more rationally. Taking into account the costs for altruistic actions in absence of material returns, altruists lose in terms of materialism in comparison to egoists that abstain from purely altruistic actions. As a result altruistic individuals as well as states have to make the decision to help only certain people and not others. Therefore, states selectively intervening for merely humanitarian purposes are in fact pure altruists and cannot be alleged of putting rationality over empathy.

In this book altruism describes an other-oriented action of states or policy-makers not motivated by self-interest but motivated by empathy or norms of morality with the sole purpose of helping individuals in need and who are not part of the own nation. The goal of improving the humanitarian situation on the ground for the sake of the suffering individuals has to be accompanied by an empathetic and benevolent motivation.

2.2.2 Idealist Approach to Humanitarian Intervention

The belief that humanitarian intervention has to follow altruistic motives and has to be borne by the propensity to help others selflessly derives from the cosmopolitan idea of moral universalism. Convinced that the world primarily consists of individuals and people rather than states, cosmopolitanism fostered the belief of a common humanity, i.e. a global society of people creating a community consisting of all individuals regardless of their affiliation to race, religion or nationality. This cosmopolitan community of people is founded upon a set of common shared

[49] Kerber (1984).

[50] Hardin (1982). (p. 167).

values of morality.[51] In this community the primary focus is directed towards the rights of individuals (human rights) while depreciating the rights of states (sovereignty) as secondary considerations. Even though the roots of cosmopolitanism can be found as early as the 18th century writings of Kant, the *de facto* global integration of states and individuals into an increasingly interdependent world towards the end of the 20th century, has strongly contributed to the consolidation of the concept of a world community. Through the erosion of the absolute state-centric worldview globalization is believed by cosmopolitans to have promoted the creation of a moral community of mankind, where the individual in one locality is directly connected to individuals in other, even remote, localities. Beyond the borders of the state or the realm of the nation individuals meet one another solely as humans and not primarily as affiliates of particular groups or nations. This presumably eradicates notions of the 'Us' and the 'Other', namely making concepts of 'fellow countryman' and 'stranger' obsolete. Thus, due to the fact that cosmopolitanism envisages a unitary world of equal individuals creating a community of common humanity, individuals are connected through universal norms, shared values, rights and duties. The primary universal norms are believed to arise from humanitarian law, granting individuals universal human rights that are to be protected and enforced by every sovereign to its people. The deprivation of basic human rights therefore constitutes not only a domestic problem, but a problem that concerns individuals and states all over the world. Hence, in cosmopolitanism, the notion of purely domestic affairs does not exist and for that reason everyone, including states, do have the moral duty to help suffering individuals anywhere. The motivation, however, to intervene has to be borne by altruistic considerations only, i.e. by a sort of philanthropic concern for a fellow human being.[52]

As a particular cosmopolitan ideology, solidarism is based on the notion of an international system consisting of states founded on a common world society that embraces the rights of individuals. Unlike pluralism that regards the international system as a mere accumulation of states, and emphasises co-existence, solidarism describes the international system primarily as a cooperative concert of states aware that individual rights have to be at the basis of this system. The solidarist worldview perceives the international community as a collective of shared values and norms, where each individual state is supposed to be committed to enforce these common values. Due to the fact that the international community manifests itself in the United Nations and due to the fact that human rights have a strong standing in the UN, the international community should invest highly in enforcing these universal rights of human beings. Therefore, intervention from a solidarist view point has to serve the sole purpose of advancing the common norms underlying the system. That is to say, since individual rights take precedence over the rights of states, intervention first of all has to have an inherent motive based on

---

51 Fixdal and Smith (1998) Op. Cit. 82 (p. 294).

52 Coates (2003). (p. 75).

solidarity: assisting individuals in need.[53] Solidarism brings forward a standpoint that asserts "[…] that […] strangers are a part of us, that security is indivisible, and that all human beings are members of one global family […]".[54] It follows that in a world society where divisions of any kind are absent, helping a fellow man is a duty for every individual and state. This duty cannot be undermined by claims describing humanitarian intervention as an allocation of resources of one nation for the sake of saving strangers from a different nation. As mankind belongs to one, indivisible society the life of a stranger becomes equal concern for every government.

Benevolence and other-oriented behaviour has been laid down in the tenets of several major religions, making altruism and charity a moral imperative. Various religions have developed a solidarist ideology. The roots for altruism in the monotheistic religions can be found in Judaism and were further developed in Christianity and Islam. Among the monotheistic religions, in particular Christianity has promoted a form of self-less altruism and charity that in its purity cannot be found in the other two religions. Arguing along the lines of solidarism, the Catholic Church has promoted a worldview that highlights the importance of solidarity among individuals, peoples and nations. As a response to the ongoing globalization of state affairs, the idea of the global village that emphasises the aspect of global interdependence and where nations are hardly immune from the effects of conduct of other nations. The Catholic Church has used these changing geo-political conditions in order to foster its decade-old commitment to the idea of the world family of common humanity.

> […] For decades the Catholic Church has championed the unity of the human family, the interdependence of peoples and the need for solidarity across national and regional boundaries. So we have welcomed the advances in communications, technology, economics and other secular forces which have brought people into ever closer contact with one another […].[55]

In papal and pastoral publications the Catholic Church has promoted a solidarist world view based on the concept of humanity as one family and the belief into a universal common good. As Pope John Paul II wrote, "[…] The very heart of international life is not so much states as man. […] There exist interests which transcend states: They are the interests of the human person, his rights […]".[56] Hence, as the former head of the Catholic Church put it, the major and primary concern of states in the international arena should be occupied with the well-being of individuals, thereby making international affairs benevolent and philanthropic. According to the United States Catholic Conference intervention must only occur for the sole reason of making the world a better place, which in some respect will lead to an improvement of one's own position. Self-interest, however, must not be

[53] Welin (2005). Op. Cit. 107 (p. 47).

[54] Ibid (p. 48).

[55] United States Catholic Conference (1992). (p. 339).

[56] John Paul (1993). (p. 587).

an incentive for states to intervene as the actual philanthropic and altruistic nature of humanitarian intervention vanishes.[57] Catholicism's approach to international relations has been based on the protection of human rights and human dignity. "[…] Stronger than the appeal of sovereignty are the human rights of persons and the obligations of solidarity […]".[58] The homocentric worldview of the Catholic Church triggers an international relations' outlook that emphasises solidarity as a core principle, i.e. empathetically assisting individuals in need for no specific material interest. Interests are not a necessary incitement due to the fact that "[…] the people of far-off lands are not abstract problems, but sisters and brothers […]".[59] Thus, altruism becomes the only virtuous approach to humanitarian intervention.

Closely linked to the Catholic approach to intervention for humanitarian purposes is the approach taken by humanitarians whose charitable actions are borne by feelings of empathy, benevolence and compassion with the misery of others. Humanitarianism "[…] means helping and protecting victims irrespective of who and where they are and why they are in need […]".[60] The overarching principle of humanitarianism is the sanctity of human life and the devotion to preserve this life. Secondary principles of importance are impartiality, consent and neutrality. Hence, humanitarians are not driven by self-interested goals but by an altruistic devotion to helping individuals in need. The dedication of humanitarianism to the altruistic assistance to people in crisis regions has a long tradition in the post-1945 world and is laid down in the principles of the International Red Cross. Pure humanitarians, however, have never been confronted with the decision to militarily intervene into another state as humanitarian organizations work as charitable NGOs solely delivering humanitarian assistance rarely interfering with the internal affairs of the receiving state. Nonetheless, NGO neutrality is often challenged when NGOs despite their outsider position take sides in a conflict.[61] With the occurrence of humanitarian intervention as a form of coercive intervention involving military capacities in the post-1990 s, humanitarians often tried to project their altruistic motivation for intervention on the intervening states despite the fact that military state intervention occurs within a different highly politicised context.[62] While NGOs enter countries often with the consent of the receiving state and under a civilian umbrella, military humanitarian intervention entails the use of force and bears the risk of losing lives, i.e. the costs of intervention are considerably higher. Nonetheless, as the term humanitarian intervention describes an intervention for humanitarian ends, humanitarians are inclined to claim that

[57] Miller (2000). (p. 21).

[58] Himes (1994). (p. 2240.

[59] United States Catholic Conference (1992). Op. Cit. 199 (p. 341).

[60] Weiss (1999). (p. 11).

[61] See Dicklitsch (1998).

[62] Ramsbotham and Woodhouse (1996). Op. Cit. 135(pp. 14–18).

humanitarian intervention has to meet the same altruistic criteria in order to do justice to its name.

Also in just war theory humanitarian intervention is commonly understood as a disinterested, rather altruistic form of intervention with the sole purpose of saving or rescuing individuals in need. Due to the fact that in a statist world system, where international law prescribes a strict adherence to the sovereignty principle, humanitarian intervention has to be regarded as an exceptional permission of the use of force. Using force for the sake of saving individuals must be detached from any ulterior interests of the intervener as not to confuse humanitarian intervention with a conventional interference into the domestic affairs of another state motivated by power considerations. Therefore, justifying humanitarian intervention in the international arena today requires the intervener to explicitly show his human-rights concerned motivation. "[…] The issue of humanitarian intervention is largely justified by viewing human rights as a jus cogens, thereby, seeing their defence as vital and warranted […]".[63] That is to say that humanitarian intervention as a contemporary *jus cogens*[64] has been accepted as an exceptional form of intervention for the purpose of the protection of human rights. The protection of human rights abroad, namely the protection of strangers abroad, is thus the internationally accepted justification of humanitarian intervention. Michael Walzer[65] stated in his prominent work *Just and Unjust Wars* already in the 1970s that intervention for humanitarian purposes can be regarded both morally and legally as an exception to the restrictive non-intervention principle. "[…] Humanitarian intervention is justified when it is a response to acts that shock moral conscience of mankind […]".[66] Thus, the existence of a supreme humanitarian emergency is the prerequisite for intervention, i.e. humanitarian intervention has to be fought primarily for humanitarian purposes. Walzer continues by arguing that

> […] We praise or don't condemn these violations of formal rules of sovereignty, because they uphold the values of individual life and communal liberty of which sovereignty itself is merely an expression […].[67]

---

[63] Helmke (2004). Op. cit. 7 (p. 13).

[64] Jus cogens =

> […]For the purposes of the present Convention, a peremptory norm of general international law is a norm accepted and recognized by the international community of States as a whole as a norm from which no derogation is permitted and which can be modified only by a subsequent norm of general international law having the same character […]

* United Nations International Law Commission. (1969). (Art. 53).

[65] Note: Despite the relatively solidarist or cosmopolitanist standpoint Walzer brings forward here, it is worth noting that his ideology continuously changed over the last decades. The standpoint taken by Walzer today might vary from the position expressed here.

[66] Walzer (1977).(p. 107).

[67] Ibid (p. 108).

The legitimacy of humanitarian intervention therefore derives from its altruistic nature, namely the concern with defending human rights. Therefore, both from a humanitarian and legal perspective, political interests should not be a driving force for intervention. Former UN High Commissioner for Refugees (UNHCR) Sadako Ogata stated in an address that

> [...] The fundamental objective of humanitarian action is to alleviate suffering and save lives. Humanitarian action focuses on people and is rights based. Political action focuses on states and is guided by national interests and respect for sovereignty [...].[68]

It follows from this remark that since humanitarian intervention is considered a humanitarian action, politics must not interfere with a decision concerned with the fate of victims who have a right of protection and relief. Realistically, however, as humanitarian intervention remains a state and thereby a political decision, the inevitable merger of politics and humanitarianism will predictably lead to a situation where the fate of suffering individuals is subject to a political and therefore amoral decision.[69]

As stated earlier in this study, Verwey (1992) and Parekh (1997) probably offer the most extreme positions towards the need for altruism in humanitarian intervention. As one of the first Verwey (1992) approached the very young concept of humanitarian intervention as a coercive action "[...] for the sole purpose of preventing or putting a halt to a serious violation of fundamental human rights [...]".[70] Parekh (1997) continues along these lines though attenuating the reference to altruism as a sole purpose by stating that humanitarian intervention is an "[...] act wholly or primarily guided by the sentiment of humanity, compassion or fellow-feeling and in that sense disinterested [...]".[71] Both authors emphasize the importance of disinterestedness as a prerequisite for intervening into the domestic affairs of another state. In fact, the motivation of the intervener has to be guided by altruism and philanthropism. Intervention is characterized as an act of great kindness whereby the intervener puts the lives of his soldiers at risk to save the lives of strangers. Richard Miller even goes that far as to state that humanitarian intervention is "[...] a form of altruism writ large, a kind of self-sacrificial love [...]".[72] For we are living in a world of common humanity, interveners should be completely other-regarding even placing the lives of strangers above the lives of own soldiers so as to ensure that intervention is determined to avert the suffering and is not solely concerned with protecting the lives of the intervening soldiers. In a more moderate way, following this argument, altruism means accepting a certain degree of risk for the own soldiers in saving strangers in need.[73]

---

68 Ogata (1998).

69 MacFarlane and Weiss (2000)(p. 112).

70 Verwey (1992). Op. Cit. 128 (p. 114).

71 Parekh (1997) Op. Cit. 130 (p. 55).

72 Miller (2000) Op. Cit. 201 (p. 17).

73 Wheeler (2004).Op. Cit. 169 (p. 5).

Commonly, altruism in humanitarian intervention is not defined in such a narrow way as not to make intervention, an obvious political endeavour, too idealistic. Humanitarian interventions are considered to be

> [...] considerably more altruistic than wars of self-defense. Such philanthropic efforts implicate few if any national interests and thus seem distant from the fiduciary duties that politicians satisfy when they marshal a war of self-defense. It is considerably easier for a national leader to garner popular support for wars of self-defense than for wars with humanitarian purposes [...].[74]

Miller defines humanitarian intervention as a philanthropic effort that realistically might feature some national interests, however, altruism has to be the foremost driving force.

References

Acharya A (2003) The War in Iraq: morality or the national interest? IDSS Commentaries. Singapore, The Institute of Defense and Strategic Studies

Atack I (2002) Ethical objections to humanitarian intervention. In: Security dialogue vol 33, no 3. Sage Publications, London

Ayoob M (2002) Humanitarian intervention and state sovereignty. Int J Hum Rights, 6(1):81–102. Routledge Publisher, London

Bar Tal D (1986). Altruistic motivation to help: definition, utility and operationalization. Humboldt J Soc Relat, 13:3–14. Humboldt State University, Areata, CA

Bellamy AJ(2003) Humanitarian intervention and the three traditions. In: Global Society, vol 17:1. Routledge Publisher London, pp 3–20

Bellamy AJ (2009) Responsibility to protect or Trojan horse? The crisis in Darfur and humanitarian intervention after Iraq. In: Rosenthal JH and Barry C (eds) Ethics and international affairs. Georgetown University Press, Washington, DC

Boettcher WA (2004) Military intervention decisions regarding humanitarian crises: framing induced risk behaviour. J Conflict Resolut, 48:331. Sage Publications, London

Buchanan A (1999) The internal legitimacy of humanitarian intervention. J Polit Philos 7(1):71–87. Wiley and Blackwell Hoboken, NJ

Chinkin C (2000) The state that acts alone: bully, good samaritan or iconoclast? Eur J Int Law, 11(1):31–41. Oxford University Press, Oxford

Coates A (2003) Humanitarian intervention: a conflict of traditions. In: Nardin, Terry and Vanessa W (eds) Humanitarian intervention. New York University Press, New York

Cook ML (2000) Immaculate war: constraints on humanitarian intervention. Ethics Int Aff 14:55–65. Carnegie Council, New York

Cooper SA (2001)Air power and the coercive use of force. Wash Q, 24(4):81–93. MIT University Press, Boston, MA

Dicklitsch S (1998) The elusive promise of NGOs in Africa: lessons from Uganda. Palgrave Macmillan, Basingstoke, UK

Dobos N (2008) Justifying humanitarian intervention for the people who pay for it. Praxis 1(1). Spring Manchester UK: Manchester University

Dobos N (2009) On altruistic war and national responsibility: justifying humanitarian intervention to soldiers and taxpayers. In: Ethical theory and moral practise. Springer, Berlin

74 Miller (2008).(p. 57).

Farer T et al (2005) Roundtable: humanitarian intervention after 9/11. Int Relat, 19:211 ff. Sage Publications on behalf of the david davies memorial institute for international studies, London

Fixdal M, Smith D (1998) Humanitarian intervention and just war. Mershon international studies review, 42(2):283–312. Hoboken, NJ: Blackwell Publishing on behalf of The international studies association

Hardin G (1982) Discriminating altruisms. Zygon, 17:163–86. Wiley and Blackwell, Hoboken, NJ

Helmke B (2004) OCEANIC—Conference on international studies. Conference papers: Humanitarian intervention: exemplifying the changing ground rules for the international use of force. Canberra, AU: ANU College of Asia and the Pacific

Himes K (1994) Catholic social thought and humanitarian intervention. In: Powers GF et al (eds) Peacemaking: moral and policy challenges for a new world. Georgetown University Press, Washington, DC

Hobbes T (1990) Vom menschen. Vom Bürger, Hamburg: Felix Meiner Verlag

John Paul II (1993) Address to the diplomatic corps. Origins 22 (Feb 4). Rugby, UK: Biblical Creation Society

Keifer BD (2003) When tactics and strategy collide. National war college report. Washington, DC: National War College, 31 Oct 2003

Kerber K (1984) The perception of nonemergency helping situation, rewards, and the altruistic personality. J Pers 52:177–187. Wiley and Blackwell Hoboken, NJ

Krauthammer C (1985) When to intervene: what's worth fighting for? The new republic vol 192. Winnipeg, CA: CanWest Global Communications, pp 10–13

Krauthammer C (1999) The short, unhappy life of humanitarian war. Natl Interest, 74:5–8. Washington, DC: National Affairs, Inc

MacFarlane SN, Weiss T (2000) Political interest and humanitarian action. Secur Stud, 10(1):112–142. Routledge, London

Maitland I (2002) The human face of self-interest. J Bus Ethics 38(1/2). At our best: Moral lives in a moral community pp 3–17. Berlin, Springer Publisher

Miller RB (2000) Humanitarian intervention, altruism, and the limits of casuistry. J Religious Ethics, 28(1):3–35. Blackwell Publishing, London

Miller RB (2008) Justifications of the Iraq war examined. Ethics Int Affairs, 22.1. Carnegie Council, New York

Morgenthau H (1985) Politics within nations, 6th edn. Knopf, New York

Nafie I (2000) An egyptian agenda, Al-Ahram Weekly. Issue No 498 Cairo: Al-Ahram, 7–13 Sep 2000

Al Jazeera. Net (2010) Bashir genocide charge under review. Al Jazeera, 3 Feb 2010. Retrieved online 22 Apr 2010 from http://english.aljazeera.net/news/africa/2010/02/201023559 20514636.html

Ogata S (1998) Keynote address. Report from the second Wolfsberg humanitarian forum, 5–7 June 1998 Geneva: International Committee of the Red Cross

Ottaway M, Lacina B (2003). International interventions and imperialism: lessons from the 1990s. SAIS Review, vol XXIII, No 2 (Summer–Fall). John Hopkins University Press, Washington D.C

Parekh B (1997) Rethinking humanitarian intervention. Int Political Sci Rev, 18(1):55–74. Sage Publications, London

Piliavin JA, Charng HW (1990) Altruism: a review of recent theory and research. Annu Rev Sociology, 16:27–65. Palo Alto, CA: Annual Reviews

Ramsbotham O, Woodhouse T (1996) Humanitarian intervention in contemporary conflict. Cambridge, UK Polity

Richardson JA (1997) Defining the post cold war national interest. Natl Forum J 1(1) Lake Charles LA: Natl Forum J

Roskin MG (1994) National interest: from abstraction to strategy. Parameters, Winter 4–18. Carlisle, PA: The US Army War College

Schwartz SH, Howard J (1984) Internalized values as motivators of altruism. In: Staub E et al (eds) Development and maintenance of pro-social behaviour: international perspectives on positive morality. Plenum, New York

Shibata MY (2006) A case study on the US policy in humanitarian intervention: Somalia, Rwanda, and Liberia. A research report (AU/ACSC/616-7978/AY06). Maxwell, AL: USAF Air University

Sid-Ahmed M (2000) The UN impasse, Al-Ahram Weekly. Issue No 479 Cairo: Al-Ahram

Slenska SD (2007) Strategy national interests and means to an end. SSI Free Publication, Carlisle, PA: The US Army War College

Smith A (1969) The theory of moral sentiments. Indianapolis: Liberty Classics

Soanes C, Stevenson A (2005) Oxford Dictionary of English, 2nd edn. Oxford University Press, Oxford

Spielvogel JJ (2004) Western civilization: a brief history: comprehensive volume. Wadsworth Publishing, Stamford, CT

United Nations International Law Commission (1969) The Vienna convention on the law of treaties. Available: Index to United Nations Documents and Publications. UN Doc. A/Conf.39/27; 1155 UNTS 331; 8 ILM 679 (1969); 63 AJIL 875 (1969)

United States Catholic Conference (1992) American responsibilities in a changing world. Origins 22.20 (Oct 29): 338–341. Rugby, UK: Biblical Creation Society

Verwey W (1992) The legality of humanitarian intervention after the cold war. In: Ferris E (ed) A challenge to intervene: a new role for the United Nations?. Life and Peace Institute, Uppsala, SE

Walzer M (1977) Just and Unjust Wars, 1st edn. Basic Books, New York

Walzer M (1995) The politics of rescue. Soc Res, 62(1):51ff. The new school of social research. New York, p 53

Weiss TG (1999) Principles, politics and humanitarian action. Ethics Int Affairs, 13:1. Carnegie Council, New York

Welin AF (2005) Minimal solidarism: post-cold war responses to humanitarian crisis. LINKÖPING UNIVERSITET. MSc in International and European Relations. Master's Thesis, Aug 2005. LIU-EKI/INT–05/022—SE. Linkoping, SE: Linkoping University

Wesley M (2005) Toward a realist ethics of intervention. Ethics Int Aff, 19.2. Carnegie Council, New York

Wheeler N (2000) Saving strangers: humanitarian intervention in international society. Oxford University Press, Oxford

Wheeler N (2004) Humanitarian intervention after 9/11. In: Anthony Lang (ed) Humanitarian intervention. Georgetown University Press Georgetown, DC

William MC (2005) What is the national interest? The neoconservative challenge in IR theory. Eur J Int Relat 11:307 ff. Sage Publications, London

Wimelius AE (2009) Humanitarian interventions as neo-colonialism? Perspectives from the Muslim world. Paper for the annual international studies association convention, March 22–25, San Diego, CA. The North–South divide and international studies. Tucson, AZ: International Studies Association

Part II
The Empirical Analysis

Chapter 3
The Motivation for Humanitarian Intervention

This chapter will analyze the actual motivating factors driving Western democracies in the post-Cold War era to use military force to halt or avert humanitarian crises. Each case of humanitarian crisis and the decision of whether to intervene or to abstain from intervention will be examined in this chapter. In particular, this chapter will clarify on basis of six variables to what extend either national/self-interests or altruism actually triggered intervention.

3.1 Research Design and Method

As the recent chapters have shown humanitarian intervention is a concept that appeared in the last two decades and has been controversially debated by members of the international law community as well as others dealing with ethics and morality in international relations. A symbiosis of the disintegration of the Eastern Bloc and globalization has paved the way for new forms of conflict as well as new forms of conflict resolution. Since humanitarian intervention has to be understood as an exception to the statist non-intervention principle of international law, this exception arguably requires a certain degree of humanitarianism or altruism to be present in order to make intervention permissible. Due to the imperfect nature of the duty to protect civilians from abuse and the ambiguous definition of this norm, humanitarian intervention remains a concept that for a great part is left to the intervening states to define.

The core question of this book, constituting the basis of the empirical approach, is whether humanitarian intervention is in fact prompted, wholly or partially, by largely altruistic or national interests-related motivations. Therefore, the following chapters will analyze both humanitarian crises of the post-1990 era that triggered intervention as well as humanitarian crises that were neglected by the international community. Even though the focus will be the motivation of the main intervener, the unit of analysis will be humanitarian interventions in general rather than state behaviour, so as to present a comprehensive and holistic answer to the question to

A. Krieg, *Motivations for Humanitarian Intervention*, SpringerBriefs in Ethics,
DOI: 10.1007/978-94-007-5374-7_3,

what degree the normative arguments presented above regarding the righteous intention and motivation for humanitarian intervention hold in real life. This book does not intend to show the varying approaches to different humanitarian crises by one state, but rather tries to give a comprehensive picture of what actually drives Western democracies to intervene in humanitarian emergencies. In the case that humanitarian crisis triggered intervention, I will focus on the motivation of the main intervener, whereas in case of non-intervention in humanitarian crisis I will analyze the motivation of the United States as the single most important and most powerful player in the international arena refraining from intervention. Unlike other countries, the US has the capabilities of deploying troops quickly and effectively all over the globe and, in addition to that, presents at least on paper a set of values that is conducive to protecting liberal values abroad.

None of the cases of intervention or non-interventions presented in this book represent a clear-cut motivation of either altruism or national-/self-interest. Rather, all of the cases present different combinations of varying degrees of altruism and of national-/self-interest. In order to analyze the incentive to intervene I will examine each case while applying a set of six parameters to each case. These six parameters consist of three altruistic and three national/self-interested parameters and attempt to depict the degree of altruism or national interest underlying the decision of states to intervene or not to intervene. Due to the fact that the interest-related parameters depict national interests in the realist sense of the word, i.e. economic and geo-strategic interests, as well as self-interests related to the decision maker of the intervening party, these three parameters will be coded as national/self-interest. In order to be able to later depict the results graphically and to facilitate systematic comparison between and within cases, each parameter is assigned a value, ranking from 0 to 5, as based on the qualitative evidence available in the particular case. The values assigned to the parameters reflect an assessment of the relative strength/ degree of the presence of the particular parameter in the humanitarian crisis. While it is acknowledged that the assignment of values is not an exact science and entails at times subjective interpretation of events, an explanation as to how the value was calculated based on the available evidence is provided. Importantly, these parameters and their values allow for a more comprehensive and systematic examination of the various factors that drove the governments in their intervention decisions, displaying the degree of national/self-interest or altruism involved.

All parameters are equally weighted as it is assumed that they are equal in terms of their influence on decisions to intervene or to abstain from intervention. Even though parameters may receive different attention by decision makers in the various intervention and non-intervention cases, the relative importance of these parameters within and in between cases is constant. Due to the fact that the values assigned to the parameters represent the extent of the existence of altruistic or self-interested factors in the crisis at hand rather than decision-making dimensions, the weighting of the parameters is not necessary to understand the availability of altruistic and self-interested motivations for the decision maker. In most cases it would be even impossible to define an accurate weighting for the parameters since for example the impact of altruistic motivations on the decision making process is still unexplored.

The parameters can be defined as follows:

Altruism

- Existence of an acute humanitarian crisis,
- Public awareness and Media Coverage,
- Feeling of moral obligation to intervene by the decision-maker.

National- /Self-Interest

- Economic interest,
- Geo-strategic interest,
- Political interest of the decision maker.

Existence of an Acute Humanitarian Crisis

A major factor having an impact on the degree of altruism involved in the decision to intervene is the actual existence of an acute humanitarian crisis. While all interventions that have been justified on basis of a humanitarian crisis present a humanitarian emergency to a certain degree, not all of them do actually meet the criterion of a supreme humanitarian emergency. I argue that the humanitarian rationale employed by the intervener must be based on an actual humanitarian crisis that goes beyond a mere human rights abuse. Thus, the crisis at hand has to be characterized as a supreme humanitarian emergency, i.e. a situation "[…] where the survival of populations and entire ethnic groups is seriously compromised […]".[1] Walzer (1977) defines a supreme emergency on basis of two components, immediacy of danger and the nature of the emergency. A supreme humanitarian emergency occurs where the danger is very immanent and its nature is of an unusual and horrifying kind.[2] The more supreme the humanitarian crisis that is utilised as a justification for intervention, the more likely the intervener is actually motivated by altruistic motives. On the contrary, the less acute or supreme the humanitarian crisis that is referred to by the intervener, the less likely the actual humanitarian crisis is the motivation for intervention. Although the argument may be made that intervention into a low scale humanitarian crisis is actually more altruistic because intervention is less morally obligatory, I claim that an intervention in a non-severe or non-acute humanitarian crisis is most likely triggered by ulterior non-altruistic motives. The reason for this is that in non-severe humanitarian crises the degree of altruism is presumably not compelling enough to trigger any intervention. I argue in this book that intervention for the sake of the suffering individuals has to be incited by a sufficiently acute and severe humanitarian crisis so as to ensure that intervention to a great extent is occupied with curing the humanitarian crisis. Apart from the existence of a supreme humanitarian emergency, also the characterization and framing of the crisis by the government is

[1] Bellamy (2004) (p.138).

[2] Walzer (1977) Op. Cit. 210 (p. 255).

an important indicator of the degree of altruism involved. It can be assumed that a government that intervenes into another country solely or primarily to avert a humanitarian crisis, will make a strong public reference to the crisis and addresses the severity of the crisis objectively. Governments that publicly condemn the humanitarian crisis prior to intervention and are not hesitant to address the full extent of the crisis are more likely to engage in an intervention that is driven by altruism due to the fact that the crisis seems to be of real concern to the policy maker. In cases where the reference to the humanitarian crisis only occurs marginally alongside other more security interested motivations, altruism is not a probable motivation. Hence, both the existence of an actual supreme humanitarian emergency together with a strong humanitarian crisis-oriented rhetoric by the government will be considered indicators for a relatively altruistic intervention. The measurements for this parameter will be expressed on basis of the following criteria:

- Severity of the humanitarian crisis
- Number of deaths
- Number of refugees
- Type of Violence (Massacre, Rape, Mutilation etc.)
- Appropriateness of government reference to the crisis
- Addressing the whole extent of the crisis promptly
- Statement that helping endangered population is the predominant cause of intervention.

Public Awareness and Media Coverage

Global media networks have become a critical actor in policy formation and have a steadily increasing impact on the decisions taken by policy makers and on public opinion. Together, public opinion and the media have merged into a strong public actor that at least in Western democracies has formed a political weight that often, if ever, cannot be disregarded by decision makers. The impact of the media on the decision of the policy maker has been defined by Feist (2001) as the 'CNN-Effect', i.e. a theory

> "[...] that compelling televisions images, such as images of a humanitarian crisis, cause [...] policy makers to intervene in a situation when such an intervention might otherwise not be in the U.S. national interest [...]"[3].

Hence, according to the 'CNN-Effect' theory interveners take a decision on basis of empathic feelings triggered by the media, which redirects the policy maker's attention away from national interest considerations towards altruistic considerations. Together with the media also public opinion, often created or shaped by the media, has a considerable impact on the policy formation of governments.

---

[3] Feist S (2001) (p. 713).

In case of strong media coverage of a humanitarian crisis a public awareness arises that may call on decision makers to do something to bring the humanitarian catastrophe to an end. Public awareness most often arises from an extensive coverage of the conflict in the media and spills over from there to a broad audience in the public, creating an empathetic call on the government to do something. Even though realists might claim that intervening in a humanitarian crisis because of public or media pressure makes the motivation self-interested, one can as well argue that strong media and public attention actually trigger a rather altruistic decision. Due to the fact that public pressure and media coverage bring a humanitarian emergency to the government's attention, governments are more likely to be inclined to intervene in a situation for an altruistic cause: saving strangers in need. Despite the fact that the motivation of the decision maker to intervene might be driven by the self-interested desire to please his electorate, the intention to intervene is altruistic, making the intervention altruistic rather than self-interested. In order to account for the relatively weak degree of self-interest involved in a decision based on public awareness, an assignment of a positive value to the parameter of 'public awareness and media coverage' on the altruistic side will also trigger an assignment of a value to the parameter of 'political interest of the decision maker' on the side of self-interest. Therefore, the parameter of public opinion and media pressure will be used as an indicator for an altruistic decision and not as an indicator for a self-interested intervention. Despite the fact that the media serves often as an independent tool creating a certain public opinion, one must not forget, that the media sometimes becomes an influential tool of policy makers to induce public opinion that is favourable to their policy goals. The latter issue will be addressed in the qualitative analysis of the cases when necessary. The measurements for this parameter will be expressed on basis of the following criteria:

- Extent of the media coverage in the particular state
- Focus of the media coverage (on the actual humanitarian crisis or not)
- Public Awareness of the crisis
- Public's attitude towards intervention.

Feeling of moral obligation to intervene by the decision-maker

Another parameter reflecting the drive of the decision maker to intervene for altruistic reasons is the personal affiliation of the decision maker with the fate of the suffering individuals on the ground. Because this parameter refers to inner motivations, the focus here will be on the decision maker at the highest state level. Even though it is difficult to find reliable sources about the state of mind of the decision maker, statements from his/her immediate vicinity can give hints about the extent to which the decision maker was empathetically engaged in the humanitarian crisis. Personal feelings of empathy and sympathy with the suffering populations abroad can be an incentive or at least a facilitator for statesmen to make an altruistic decision towards intervention. Personal experiences of the past, personal ethics or even personal affiliations with certain groups can lead decision-makers to make altruistic decisions in favour of others. The measurements for this parameter will be expressed on basis of the following criteria:

- Number of reliable statements that decision maker felt empathetic with endangered population
- Depth of empathy with the endangered population
- Credibility of the expressed statement.

Economic interest

One of the prime indicators of a self-interested or national interest based motivation is the presence of economic interests for the intervening states. That is to say, that when the receiving state offers a broad range of important natural resources or crucial trade routes that are vital to the national interests of the intervening state, the intervener might decide to intervene not only to avert the humanitarian crisis but also to secure mineral exploitation rights for domestic companies. In particular when the receiving state is a key producer of strategic resources such as oil, intervention in humanitarian crises bares the potential of ulterior motives. The existence of economic interests in a region can usually be proven after the intervention occured as it becomes obvious how the intervening country has facilitated access to resources and trading routes to domestic companies. While most of the time economic interests only affect governments indirectly since these interests oftentimes primarily serve domestic companies, sometimes in case of a threat to continuous supply of existentially important resources such as fossil fuels, it is the direct interest of the government to secure sufficient supplies for the home market even if it entails coercion. The measurements for this parameter will be expressed on basis of the following criteria:

- Availability of vital natural resources
- Strategic importance of crisis region for regional or global trade.

Geo-strategic interest

In this study geo-strategic interests are defined as security-related national interests that are either threatened in close proximity to the national mainland or in regions of particular national interests abroad. The term 'geo-strategic interest' reflects the connection between power, security and geographical space in the international arena. In this respect power refers to influence and control over territory and resources, while security refers to the protection of the own territory and territory of particular interests from foreign influence. Thus, when conflicts threaten vital national interests in a particular country or threaten to spill-over to regions of vital national interest, it is in the geo-strategic interest of this particular nation to bring this conflict to an end. Particularly conflicts that erode the authority structure and the administrative infrastructure of a state, pose a threat to Western democracies as the resulting failed states might become safe havens for terrorists or sub-state military structures that operate within the freedom of lawlessness. Therefore, intervening for geo-strategic interests means to secure the safety of one's nation not only in the close proximity to the national borders but also to protect the nation abroad. In order to secure strategic military positions or retain control over a strategically important locality, Western democracies, predominantly the United States, have been engaged in changing hostile regimes. Even though Western democracies make it look as if regime change as well as the spread of liberal values and democracy are an altruistic act of benevolence, it is obvious that Western commitment to the installation or restoration of a pro-Western regime does primarily serve their own national interests before it serves the interests of the people living under these regimes.[4] Further, also the dedication to internationalism, i.e. the support for and participation in popular struggles for self-determination, has to be understood as a motive on basis of geo-strategic interest due to the fact that Western regimes believe that like-minded regimes (equally founded on values such as democracy and liberalism) are more supportive partners in international relations. Hence, the support of national liberation struggles is only of altruistic nature if liberation is a local initiative supported by the majority of people living in the country.[5] Imposing liberal values and democracy on countries as a response to a humanitarian catastrophe merely serves the geo-strategic interests of the intervening state. Thus, fighting security threats abroad, altering the nature of regimes abroad or enhancing one's own power status in relation to others are actions serving geo-strategic interests. The measurements for this parameter will be expressed on basis of the following criteria:

Presence of security interests

- Vital region in war on terror
- State poses a threat to intervening state.

Presence of strategic interests

- Facilitate Consolidation of Influence in Strategically Important Region
- Potential of Spill-Over of Conflict and Threat to Integrity and Stability of the Region.

Political Interest of the Decision Maker

The last parameter which also serves as an indicator for a self-interested decision to intervene is the political interest of the decision maker, i.e. his or her expected gains or losses from intervention/non-intervention in the domestic political realm. Due to the fact that in this book I analyze decisions of liberal democracies to intervene or abstain from intervention, the political repercussions of any intervention decision are a decisive factor in the decision making process. As the political career of decision makers, particularly in democracies, is highly

[4] Ottaway and Lacina (2003) Op. Cit. 56 (p. 86).

[5] Walzer (1995) Op. Cit. 1 (p. 55).

dependent on the support of the electorate, statesmen are constantly inclined to make decisions in favour of public will. When interventions seem to contribute to the creation of a positive image of the decision maker domestically, the political interest of the decision maker will trigger intervention. On the contrary, when intervention is not conducive to the public stance of the decision maker, intervention will most likely not occur. Further, since military intervention is a rather sensitive issue domestically, intervention can also serve the ends of diverting public attention away from other domestic issues threatening to generate a negative image of the policy maker. Thus, the political interest of the decision maker can serve as a facilitator and even as a motivation for intervention, making the decision to intervene more self-interested. The measurements for this parameter will be expressed on basis of the following criteria:

- Potential of diverting public attention away from domestic issues towards foreign issues by humanitarian intervention
- Mounting public pressure
- Potential for decision-maker to boost his position in upcoming elections.

3.2 Case Analysis

In the following section the various intervention and non-intervention cases will be qualitatively analyzed on basis of six different parameters. The score of the quantitative value, ranging from 0 to 5, will be generated based on the available qualitative evidence and will appear as a numerical value next to the individual parameter. This numerical value will allow comparing the degree of altruism as well as national interests within and between cases and parameters.

3.2.1 Northern Iraq (Operation Provide Comfort, *1991)*

The victory of coalition forces over the Iraqi army in the Gulf War was followed by an unsuccessful attempt of Kurdish and Shiite forces to overthrow the regime of Saddam Hussein. After the uprisings failed, in particular Kurds in Northern Iraq began to flee from their homes in fear of government retaliation. In the beginning of April 1991 about one million refugees had fled into the mountainous border region between Iraq and Turkey as well as Iran.[6] Confronted with 10,000–30,000 casualties within a few weeks, the Security Council released UN SC Resolution 688 (1991) insisting "[...] that Iraq allow immediate access by international humanitarian organizations to all those in need of assistance in all parts of Iraq and

[6] Jakobsen (1996) (p. 208).

to make available all necessary facilities for their operation [...]".[7] Despite the fact that the Security Council did not explicitly authorize an intervention, a coalition under the leadership of the United States used the 'overwhelming humanitarian need' as a justification to intervene and set up safe havens and no-fly zones in Northern Iraq and later in Southern Iraq.[8] Further, the fact that SC Resolution 688 (1991) stated that the continuous refugee flows in the border region were threatening international peace and security contributed to the legitimization of the intervention. Due to the fact that the US was the main intervener (5,000 troops) I will focus in this research on the US motivation and intention.

Existence of an acute humanitarian crisis [2,5]

The operations by the Iraqi regime trying to put down the rebellion in Northern Iraq caused a dramatic refugee stream moving towards Turkey. Turkey sealed the borders as the Turkish government felt incapable of dealing with such a huge number of refugees and the potential security risk Kurds might pose to the regional stability in the Turkish border region. As a result more than a million displaced Kurds were languishing in Northern Iraq, exposed to the approaching Iraqi government forces. Under the war-like circumstances humanitarian organizations were unable to properly access the conflict region in order to feed the starving population. Bad weather conditions and starvation caused death rates of up to 1,000 individuals daily, killing between 10,000 and 30,000 individuals within a few weeks.[9] Democratic Congressman Hamilton declared that Iraqi helicopters "[...] are now creating a bloodbath [...]"[10] indicating the severity of the situation on the ground. Thus, the humanitarian crisis was severe and it became clear that continuing to remain passive would increase the death rate sharply, making the crisis acute. Even though the Bush administration did not respond instantly and adequately, Secretary of State Baker announced after witnessing the humanitarian crisis in the refugee camps that "[...] these people must be free from the threats, persecution and harassment that they have been subjected to by that brutal regime in Baghdad [...]".[11] After returning to the US, Baker declared that the administration could no longer stand by leaving the Kurds dying on the mountains of Northern Iraq. Thus, the Bush administration responded by intervening for humanitarian reasons after witnessing an actual acute humanitarian crisis. The official reference to the supreme humanitarian emergency by the government, however, was rather weak since it failed to address the crisis using the right terminology. For the most part, US officials referred to the crisis as just another civil war without speaking of severe human rights abuses.

---

[7] UN Security Council Op. Cit. 55.

[8] Roberts (1993) Op. Cit. 19 (p. 436).

[9] Ryter (2003) Op. Cit. 17 (p. 37).

[10] FT (1991).

[11] Wheeler (2002) Op. Cit. 54 (p. 148).

Public Awareness and Media Coverage [3,5]

Despite the fact that the Bush administration decided initially to leave the Kurds to themselves as their struggle was perceived as a long-standing internal conflict that had to be resolved without the risk of deploying US troops, the 400–1,000 fatalities daily triggered international media attention.[12] The increasing media attention throughout April 1991 caused the crisis to appear on the agenda of the Western states, particularly grasping the attention of political decision makers as well as public opinion. It has been widely argued that the 'CNN–effect' had a decisive impact on the decision making of the Bush administration.[13] The relentless and emotive coverage of the suffering of the Kurdish people trapped on the border to Turkey and Iran reached such a climax that the Bush administration had 'to do something'[14]. Following the intensive media coverage the American public still wrapped up with the overwhelming victory during Operation Desert Storm began to shift their focus to the resulting humanitarian crisis in Northern Iraq. Bush's initial reluctance to jeopardize American troops in an internal conflict abroad triggered the formation of a strong public support for an intervention for the fate of the suffering Kurdish population. Public opinion pressure and a feeling of strong public solidarity with the plight of the Kurdish refugees became important factors for the Bush administration to contemplate an intervention for the sake of saving suffering individuals abroad.[15] Thus, one can state that both intensive media coverage together with an empathetic public opinion made possible or at least facilitated a rather altruistic decision in favour of the endangered Kurds in Northern Iraq.

Feeling of moral obligation to intervene by the decision-maker [1]

President Bush was initially convinced that intervention for humanitarian purposes would be politically counterproductive for him since he apparently believed that the deployment of US troops would not be accepted by the American public. Nonetheless President Bush appears to have been emotionally touched by the images of suffering Kurds. "[…] Well, I feel frustrated any time innocent civilians are being slaughtered. And I feel very frustrated about that […]"[16] he stated speaking after the UN SC Resolution 688 (1991) was passed on April 5th. This statement demonstrates that President Bush at least to a minor extent was emotionally moved by the images of starving Kurds. Further, President Bush among many Western leaders may have felt responsible for the suffering Kurds as it was the Western coalition's intervention during Operation Desert Storm that created the humanitarian crisis: In as much as the US administration had unsuccessfully incited the rebellion of the Kurds against Hussein's regime, President Bush may

12 Ibid (p. 147).

13 Jakobsen (1996) Op. cit. 224 (p. 208).

14 Mandelbaum (1994). (p. 16)

15 Kirisçi (1996) (p. 21).

16 Quoted in Stuckey (1992).

have been driven at least to some degree by a sense of moral obligation to help the suffering Kurds.[17]

Economic interest [0]

Unlike during Operation Desert Strom evidence of economic interests of the United States in the particular area of Northern Iraq could not be found. Solely focusing on the rather resource-poor region of Northern Iraq and disregarding the fossil fuel-abundant South of the country, the intervention to save Kurds in the North did not directly serve the protection of economic interests.

Geo-strategic interest [4]

Traditionally the US has a very strong interest in the regional security and stability of the Middle East. The humanitarian crisis in April 1991 had the potential to weaken the stability of the region both affecting Turkey and Iran. More than one million people were displaced in Northern Iraq and put pressure on the Turkish government that was reluctant to allow an influx of Kurds so as not to change the demographic reality in Southern Turkey. Helplessly the Turkish government that had supported the US intervention during Operation Desert Storm and that was a key NATO ally in the region called on the Bush administration for help.[18] Thus, the US intervention was certainly also driven by the fear of a spill-over of the Kurdish conflict to one of its most important allies in the region, making the humanitarian crisis also a geo-political state of emergency.[19] Apart from that, also Saudi Arabia expressed its concern that Iran might get involved in the crisis in order to secure its borders with the Kurdish regions in Northern Iraq as well as to support the Shiite uprisings in the South.[20] Thus, due to the fact that both key allies Turkey and Saudi Arabia supported the US-led intervention to Iraq during Operation Desert Storm and both were threatened by geo-political changes of power relations in the region, the US was inclined to intervene so as to uphold security and stability in a region of vital national interest.

Political interest of the decision maker [1]

The decision maker, i.e. President Bush and his administration, did not receive any personal political advantages from the intervention. Though, the strong public pressure for an altruistic intervention in Northern Iraq motivated the decision to intervene at least partially due to the fact that neither Bush nor other members of cabinet could afford to conduct foreign policy against the will of the electorate. Secretary of State Baker's visit to Iraq during the onset of the crisis shows that

---

17 Roberts (1993) Op. Cit. 19 (p. 437).

18 MacFarlane and Weiss (2000) Op. Cit. 213 (p. 127).

19 Livingston (1997) (p. 10).

20 Wheeler (2002) Op. Cit. 54 (p. 148).

apparently there must have been a sense in Washington that it might be politically beneficial 'to do something' rather than standing by passively.[21]

Operation *Provide Comfort* in Northern Iraq presents a relatively balanced motivation, comprised of both altruistic and self-interested components. The existence of a humanitarian crisis, media coverage, public opinion and Bush's personal compassionate feelings played into the decision making in the same way as geo-strategic and political interests. Nevertheless, the motivation to intervene in Northern Iraq appears to be overall more altruistic than national interest based.

3.2.2 Somalia (Operation **Restore Hope,** *1992)*

After the pro-Western President Siad Barre was overthrown by rebel groups in 1991, Somalia slid into a power vacuum that could not be filled by any of the rivalling rebel groups. By the end of the year 1991 the various clans were fighting each other heavily, destroying agricultural and life stock production all over the country. The resultant famine killed more than 350,000 people by 1992 while foreign aid supplies were used by the rebel groups to put pressure on the population and NGOs on the ground. The inflowing humanitarian aid was seized by militias to sell food supplies to the starving population in return for public support for their cause.[22] In response to the ongoing crisis the UN Security Council adopted UN SC Resolution 794 (1992) declaring that "[…] the magnitude of the human tragedy caused by the conflict in Somalia, further exacerbated by the obstacles being created to the distribution of humanitarian assistance, constitutes a threat to international peace and security […]".[23] Therefore, UN SC Resolution 794 (1992) allowed Member States "[…] to use all necessary means to establish […] a secure environment for humanitarian relief operations […]".[24] Hence, the Security Council for the first time authorized intervention for humanitarian purposes under Chapter VII of the UN Charter. On December 9th, 1992 the first US troops landed on the beaches of Mogadishu commencing Operation *Restore Hope*. As the US was the main intervening power I will focus on the US motivation to intervene.

Existence of an acute humanitarian crisis [4,5]

More than one and a half years of civil war and seizure of foreign aid supplies had created a status of a severe humanitarian emergency in Somalia. In October 1992 75 % of the entire population of 6 million Somalis were threatened by severe malnutrition, whereby 1.5 million people, particularly children, were at immediate

---

[21] Ibid.

[22] Ibid (p. 176).

[23] UN Security Council (1992).

[24] Ibid.

mortal risk. The International Committee of the Red Cross declared that even a third of the entire population, i.e. 2 million people, were in imminent danger of dying of starvation if the foreign food supplies continued to fail to arrive at their destination.[25] The experience of more than 350,000 famished Somalis within 11 months, a daily death toll of more than 1,000 Somalis and the prospect of even more severe food shortages over the winter made the humanitarian crisis at hand highly acute.[26] Thus, the humanitarian situation in Somalia towards the end of 1992 was arguably one of the most severe and acute humanitarian crises in the 1990s. Until July 1992 the Bush administration remained silent about the humanitarian crisis at hand. Only when Bush was informed about the magnitude of the suffering on the ground in July 1992 he initiated the delivery of tons of food supplies. In August 1992 Bush announced in Congress "[…] that „starvation in Somalia is a major human tragedy "and that the US would provide food for „those who desperately need it […]".[27] Thus, despite the fact that the US administration remained silent for a year, Bush took initiative as soon as he heard about the severity of the 'tragedy'.[28] Realizing that shipping food to Somalia alone would not relieve the situation, the administration decided to send troops to support the humanitarian effort of NGOs. In his address to the nation on December 4th, 1992 Bush stated that the mission of Operation *Restore Hope* was humanitarian and concerned with the protection of the lives of suffering Somalis.[29] Thus, the Bush administration clearly made a reference to the humanitarian crisis, making it the paramount purpose of intervention to stop the humanitarian crisis.

Public Awareness and Media Coverage [2,5]

Despite common belief that Operation *Restore Hope* coined the term 'CNN-effect' due to the apparent strong media coverage propelling the US administration to act,[30] research in recent years has demonstrated that the impact of the media on the decision to intervene was not as strong. From the outbreak of the crisis in January 1991 until November 1992 media coverage of the conflict was marginal at best. The media only began to cover the story increasingly after information leaked that the US administration was thinking about the possibility of intervening in the crisis at the end of November 1992. After months of political debate behind closed doors President Bush agreed on an NSC meeting on November 25th 1992 to offer 28,000 troops to the UN in order to bring to a hold the humanitarian crisis. Suddenly the media attention shifted away from the election campaigns towards the crisis in Somalia broadcasting expressive and graphic pictures of the misery on

25 Lofland (2003) (p. 56).

26 Ryter (2003) Op. Cit. 17 (p. 40).

27 Pilger (1993).

28 Glanville (2005) (p. 3).

29 Bush (1992).

30 Mandelbaum (1994) Op. Cit. 232 (p. 16).

the ground.[31] Secretary of State at the time Lawrence Eagleburger nonetheless argued afterwards that

> [...] *television had a great deal to do with President Bush's decision to go in. I was one of those two or three that was strongly recommending he do it, and it was very much because of the television pictures of these starving kids* [...].[32]

Hence, one can argue that the media did not initiate the debate for intervention, however, supported the decision to act to save the starving population once Bush had announced that intervention was a possibility. The arising strong coverage of the conflict in the beginning of December 1992 certainly facilitated public support for Bush's decision to intervene and risk American soldiers' lives for saving strangers since the American public was emotionally touched by the expressive pictures of hundreds of thousands of starving Somalis. An opinion poll conducted by The New York Times/CBS revealed that 81 % of the respondents agreed that the government is doing the right thing in sending troops to Somalia to ensure that food arrives where it is needed. 70 % of the respondents agreed that the mission was even worth the possible loss of American lives.[33] Thus, against common belief the media played only a facilitating role in making an altruistic decision, endorsing public support for an other-oriented intervention.[34]

Feeling of moral obligation to intervene by the decision-maker [4]

The images of suffering Somalis and dying children affected President Bush very personally. Andrew Natsios recalls a meeting that he attended between Bush and CARE-US director Johnson in December 1992 where Bush described a visit that he and his wife had made in the 1980s to a shelter for starving children in Sudan. Bush declared that the memories of the suffering he had witnessed there stoutly affected his decision to send troops to Somalia.[35] Further, Bush said in this meeting that "[...] No one should have to die at Christmas" (Bush said)[...] It's not more complicated than that [...]",[36] expressing his personal empathy with starving individuals fostered by the rather charitable ambience of Christmas. John Woods recalls that

> [...] *It was truly his* [Bush] *personal decision, based in large measure on his growing feelings of concern as the humanitarian disaster continued to unfold relentlessly despite the half measures being undertaken by the international community* [...].[37]

---

31 Robinson (2001) (p. 949).

32 Wheeler (2002) Op. Cit. 54 (p. 180).

33 Durch (1996) (p. 320).

34 The media may actually have been used by the government to endorse public support. Nonetheless, both the media and public opinion helped promoting an other-oriented, altruistic decision.

35 Natsios (1996) (p. 168).

36 DiPrizio (2002) (p. 60).

37 Woods (1997) (p. 158).

Therefore, it becomes apparent that Bush's personal feelings of compassion to a large extent triggered an altruistic decision.

Economic Interest [1,5]

Although the literature describes the intervention in Somalia as "[...] the first war that has not been waged in the name of 'national interests', but rather in the name of principles and values [...]"[38] evidence can be found that suggests that economic interests might have played a role in deciding in favour of intervention. An article by Mark Fineman that appeared in the LA Times in January 1993 claims that intervention actually served the interest of four American petroleum giants that had exploitation contracts with the Barre regime before the crisis, allocating two-thirds of Somalia's oil to these American conglomerates. Solving the crisis and restoring peace and stability was in the interest of the American oil giants Conoco, Amoco, Chevron and Phillips whose multi-million dollar investments were threatened by the civil war. The fact that US troops used premises of Conoco as their base and as their operational headquarters supports, according to Fineman, the claim that the Bush administration was at least partially motivated to intervene due to the pressure from oil lobbyists. Further, it was President Bush himself, who as a former Texas oilman advocated the investments of American oil companies in the state near the oil-rich Gulf of Aden.[39] Thus, it seems likely that President Bush in fact sought to kill two birds with one stone when he intervened in Somalia, helping the suffering population as well as advancing US economic interests.

Geo-Strategic Interest [0]

US geo-strategic interests in Somalia were hard to find in 1992/93. The end of the Cold War as well as technological innovations had made the US Air Force base Berbara (Somalia) obsolete and caused its dismantlement in 1991. Somalia had become insignificant for the US regional strategic interests.[40] Apart from that, the way the operation was conducted suggests that it was not intended to re-stabilize the country for the long run in as much as the mission initially did not focus on the disarmament of the militias. Such a move would have been essential if the creation of a strategic foothold in the region was intended.[41] Moreover, in the pre-9/11 world a failed state was not yet regarded a threat as a potential safe haven for terrorist activities. Therefore, while Somalia might be of geo-strategic interest today for the War on Terror, these considerations most likely did not play into the decision making in 1992.

[38] Havel (1999) (p. 6).

[39] Fineman (1993).

[40] Somalia was not of geo-strategic importance for the US in 1992 as it had lost its significance in the East–West conflict, the Somalia civil war did not threaten the water ways passing the Horn of Africa and local Islamic tendencies did not pose a threat to the US homeland, yet.

[41] Finnemore (2003) Op. Cit. 22 (p. 55).

Political Interest of the Decision Maker [4]

The upcoming elections (November 3rd, 1992) had a decisive bearing on the decision to intervene since the debate on the policy towards Somalia became an integral part of the election campaigns. Throughout the campaign President Bush was repeatedly accused by Democratic candidate Clinton of having neglected crises abroad such as those in Somalia and Bosnia. In fact Bush was reproached for foreign policy failures over these two crises. In order to silence his critiques Bush initiated the humanitarian relief operation to send aid to starving Somalis in August 1992, a move that can be understood as the first step to the military intervention later on.[42] Once defeated in the elections, partially due to the apparent lack of foreign policy successes during his Presidency, President Bush was eager to take the opportunity in December 1992 to end his Presidency on a moral high note.[43] Bush's concern for his presidential legacy certainly contributed to his decision to intervene. Not having done enough in Bosnia, Somalia offered the possibility for him to repair his foreign policy reputation by saving a considerable amount of people. A Defence Department Official stated that "[…] I had the feeling that no matter what was said (by his advisors), he [Bush] would not want to leave office with 50,000 people starving that he could have saved […]".[44] Hence, the intervention in Somalia was to a large degree incited by Bush's personal and political interest. The political debate surrounding the election campaign 1992 had painfully shown Bush that his Presidency was not marked by successful foreign policy initiatives causing him to first of all initiate a humanitarian relief operation to win the elections and after the elections defeat, causing him to send troops to Somalia in order to save his reputation.

Operation *Restore Hope* in Somalia refutes any realist claim that altruism in international relations is a utopian concept. The intervention in Somalia was the most altruistic intervention for humanitarian purposes in the post-Cold War era, presenting a motivation that was comprised by two-thirds of altruistic considerations and only by one third of interest-related considerations. In absence of geo-strategic interests and the presence of only minimal economic interests, only the political interests of Bush taint the picture of an otherwise altruistic intervention.

3.2.3 Haiti (Operation **Uphold Democracy,** *1994)*

On September 30th 1991 the first democratically elected President of Haiti, Aristide, was overthrown by a military junta led by General Cédras. The ensuing political persecution under the terror of the military regime led to an exodus of

---

42 Wheeler (2002) Op. Cit. 54 (p. 180).

43 Wheeler (2003) (p. 39).

44 Glanville (2005) Op. Cit. 246 (p. 5).

thousands of Haitians fleeing the island nation towards the shores of the United States. Initially President Bush responded to the situation by declaring a trade embargo. The following year international pressure and increasing political and economic isolation of Haiti failed to persuade the military junta to step down and to bring the arising humanitarian crisis to an end. In July 1993 both parties, President Aristide and General Cédras, came to an agreement that the junta was to resign and allow Aristide to return to power by October 1993. The agreement, however, was never implemented and the newly elected President Clinton had to realize that the crisis could only be solved by more coercive means.[45] The failure of economic sanctions and international mediation finally led to UN Security Council Resolution 940 (1994) authorizing the USA

> [...] *to use all necessary means to facilitate the departure from Haiti of the military leadership* [...] *the prompt return of the legitimately elected President and the restoration of the legitimate authorities of the Government of Haiti* [...].[46]

With a 20,000-man intervention force on the way, a trio consisting of former President Carter, former Chairman of the Joint Chiefs of Staff Powell, and Senate Armed Services Committee Chairman Nunn, succeeded in convincing the junta to give up before the actual violent clash of armed forces.[47]

Existence of an acute humanitarian crisis [3]

After the coup d'état of the military junta the humanitarian situation on the ground in Haiti deteriorated rapidly as the new leaders began to force political support by intimidating the civilian population. The number of human rights abuses increased drastically while Cédras' regime began to eliminate political opposition through murder, physical mutilation, rape and the confiscation of property. During the almost three years of the military dictatorship approximately 4,000 Haitians were systematically killed by the regime.[48] In addition to that, the looting of the Haitian economy by the military junta caused shortages of vital goods leading to starvation and malnourishment. These inhumane conditions forced tens of thousands of Haitians to flee the country and to seek refuge on US territory. Within the first six months after the putsch more than 35,000 refugees arrived in the US creating a humanitarian burden on the US government.[49] The humanitarian situation in Haiti was unbearable and acute despite the fact that the fatality rate might indicate a lower severity level than in the cases presented earlier in this book. In his address to the nation from September 15, 1994 President Clinton condemned the military regime in Haiti as a "[...] a nightmare of bloodshed [...]" characterized by "[...] a

---

45 Edwards (2008) (p. 839).

46 UN Security Council (1994a) (p. 2).

47 Jakobsen (1996) Op. Cit. 224 (p. 211).

48 CJA (2009).

49 Grünholz (2005) (p. 84).

horrible intimidation campaign of rape, torture and mutilation […]".[50] Clinton continues by stating that "[…] Cédras and his armed thugs have conducted a reign of terror, executing children, raping women, killing priests […]".[51] Hence, both the actual existence of an acute humanitarian crisis and the explicit condemnation of this crisis by the President suggest that the core motivation for intervention was to bring the humanitarian crisis to an end.

Public Awareness and Media Coverage [2]

The media coverage of the crisis in Haiti intensified after thousands of Haitian refugees landed in the US and the US media started to explore the story behind this great exodus. The media focus was particularly directed towards the person of General Cédras and his military junta, which was presented as a group of violent thugs. Covering the individual misery of the refugees arriving in the US and developing the background story about the inhumane reign of the military junta forcing the country deeper and deeper into economic ruin, the US media created public awareness for the crisis in Haiti.[52] The escalating human rights abuses in Haiti and the developing refugee crisis at home pressured the US government to take action. However, despite the consent in the US public that something needed to be done, the use of force to restore democracy and bring the humanitarian crisis to an end was strongly opposed by the US public. President Clinton's attempt to convince the US public that America should take over responsibility for the restoration of democracy in Haiti was unsuccessful. On the eve of military intervention an opinion poll revealed that 60 % of Americans opposed the deployment of US soldiers in Haiti while only 31 % were in favour of intervention.[53] Hence, before and throughout the intervention, US public opinion remained sceptical about the necessity of military intervention, though it was compassionate with the suffering Haitians.[54] Coverage by the media may have contributed to the administration's support for an intervention for the benefit of the Haitians, but media coverage did not succeed in winning over public opinion as the public did not consider the crisis severe enough to risk the lives of American soldiers.

Feeling of moral obligation to intervene by the decision-maker [0]

Despite the fact that Clinton's public statements regarding the crisis suggest that he was emotionally touched by the atrocities committed by the junta in Haiti, it remains questionable to what extent these statements qualify as evidence of personal feelings to be morally obliged to intervene. Any credible private statements/notes explicitly addressing the crisis and his personal feelings could not be found.

---

50 Clinton (1994).

51 Ibid.

52 Goddard (1997) (p. 5).

53 Rudolf (2000) (p. 315).

54 Martin (1997) (p. 7).

Therefore, Clinton's personal emotional involvement in the crisis remains a mere assumption.

Economic Interest [3]

Due to the fact that Haiti constituted an impoverished state without any noteworthy economic production or vital trade hub, the economic significance of Haiti for the United States was peripheral at best.[55] Nonetheless, Mike Blakely (1999) argues that economic interests were an important driving force initiating the US government to intervene in Haiti. Within almost three years of humanitarian crisis the United States had become the main target for refugees from Haiti, creating serious humanitarian costs for the US government. According to Blakely "[…] the Clinton administration used cost savings as an explicit rationale for intervention […]".[56] In fact, consistent with estimates, the costs for rescue and diversion of Haitian seaborne refugees as well as for the accommodation of refugees added up to approximately $ 500 million dollars prior to the intervention. The costs in the months immediately before the intervention made up $ 63 million alone.[57] Hence, with the prospect of a deterioration of the humanitarian situation in Haiti and even more refugees to come, an intervention in order to ameliorate the situation appeared to be a cost-efficient solution to the problem.

Geo-Strategic Interest [3]

The coup d'état brought a military junta to power in Haiti that threatened to destabilize the entire Caribbean region, a region of vital American security interests. The economic downturn in Haiti and the enormous exodus of Haitian refugees to proximate territories had the potential to spill over to other states in the Caribbean. Due to the fact that the Haitian crisis did not take place in a remote locality far away from the US homeland but instead in its immediate vicinity made the crisis, according to the Monroe Doctrine, a problem in America's own region.[58] Further, as Clinton stated in his address to the nation on September 15th 1994, the US had to endorse its security interests that partially consisted of "[…] promot[ing] democracy in our hemisphere […]".[59] Thus, regime restoration was an explicit motivation for the Clinton administration to intervene in Haiti. Notwithstanding the fact that democracy promotion appears to be a universalistic motivation or even altruistic motivation,[60] it actually serves the interests of the regime changer. Thus, the restoration of a democratic regime in the Western hemisphere was partially a self-interested act of the US reinstalling a friendly

[55] Mandelbaum (1996) (p. 22).

[56] Blakely (1999) (p. 92).

[57] Ibid (p. 103).

[58] Goddard (1997) Op. Cit. 270 (p. 6).

[59] Clinton (1994) Op. cit. 268.

[60] Gleddisch et al. (1997) (p. 13).

pro-American regime in Haiti.[61] Since the reinstallation of Aristide facilitated US influence over the Caribbean the regime change was certainly within the US geo-strategic interest.

Political Interest of the Decision Maker [3]

The decision to intervene in the humanitarian crisis in Haiti in 1994 was also driven by particular personal interests of President Clinton who had started his Presidency with two foreign policy failures. After initially refusing to bomb Bosnia and first sending, then withdrawing, troops from Somalia, President Clinton had earned a reputation for inconsistency. Haiti offered him the opportunity to compensate for the two failures by determinately enforcing US foreign policy goals.[62] Moreover, Clinton was haunted by the upcoming midterm elections of 1994. US voters would be deciding about the political future of Clinton based on two foreign policy failures.[63] Bearing in mind that Clinton had presented himself as a political leader with high foreign policy ambitions during his campaign two years earlier, Haiti gave Clinton the chance to repair his political image.

After the disenchantment of the notion of bloodless humanitarian intervention in Somalia a year earlier, it appears as if the intervention in Haiti constitutes the end for overall altruistic interventions. Realizing the substantial costs in man and material connected to humanitarian intervention, it seems as if Clinton had to become more careful not to rush into another military engagement lacking any substantial national interests. Clinton remained hesitant to allocate troops and funds to the crisis until the costs of non-intervention became that high that intervention appeared to be a sensible and cost-efficient alternative. Therefore, Operation *Uphold Democracy* presents an overall self-interested motivation with a much weaker altruistic component than the previous humanitarian interventions in Northern Iraq or Somalia.

3.2.4 Rwanda (Operation **Turquoise**, *1994)*

Three years of civil war in Rwanda between the two major ethnic groups, the Hutu and the Tutsi, had been brought to an end by the international community with the signature of the Arusha Accords in 1993. Instead of soothing tensions, deeply rooted in a history of hatred and aggression between the Hutu and Tutsi, the Arusha Accords added fuel to the fire as they were badly mediated and did not satisfy the demands of both parties.[64] In the months following the signature of the

[61] Ottaway and Lacina (2003) Op. cit. 56 (p. 87).

[62] Mandelbaum (1994) Op. Cit. 273 (p. 18).

[63] Robyn (2001) (p. 20).

[64] Lemarchand (2006) (p. 6).

Accords, the UN Peacekeeping Force UNAMIR,[65] which was deployed to supervise the implementation of the Accords, witnessed increasing tensions between the ethnic groups. Despite warnings by UNAMIR's General Dallaire that militias supported by the Hutu government were preparing genocide against the Tutsis, the international community did little to act. When Hutu President Habyarimana's plane was shot down over Kigali Airport on April 6th 1994, the retained aggression and hatred against the Tutsis erupted into a genocide aiming at the extinction of the entire Tutsi population.[66] Rather than living up to their mandate to protect civilians, the UN decided to reduce UNAMIR's strength to 270 troops, and General Dallaire had to stand by passively watching hundreds of thousands of Tutsis getting slaughtered.[67] Only three months after the eruption of hostilities and after hundreds of thousands were killed, the French government agreed to intervene and create a safe-haven for refugees. UN Security Council Resolution 929 (1994) authorized the French Operation *Turquoise* to use "[...] all necessary means to achieve the humanitarian objectives [...]".[68] On June 22nd 1994 a force comprising 2,500 French soldiers and 500 troops from seven African states established a safe haven in Rwanda. This section will analyze the decision of the French government to intervene.[69]

Existence of an acute humanitarian crisis [3]

The genocide in Rwanda certainly satisfied the criteria for a supreme humanitarian emergency as "[...] the survival of populations and entire ethnic groups [was] seriously compromised [...]".[70] Within three months more than 800,000 people were slaughtered using primitive weapons such as machetes, making it the worst genocide in terms of casualties per months in the history of mankind.[71] In fact it is commonly acknowledged that "[...] the most remarkable aspect of the genocide was its speed [...]".[72] In addition to the vitiation of more than 11 % of the entire population within weeks more than 2 million individuals were displaced seeking refuge in the neighbouring states of the Great Lakes region.[73] Thus, without a doubt the humanitarian crisis in Rwanda in the first two months constituted an acute humanitarian catastrophe. However, by the time the French government decided to intervene in June 1994 the genocide was almost over and the situation

---

65 UNAMIR = United Nations Assistance Mission for Rwanda.

66 Grünfeld (2007) Op. cit. 64 (p. 92).

67 Barnett (2002) (p. 76).

68 UN Security Council (1994b) (p. 2).

69 In the Humanitarian Intervention literature the genocide in Rwanda 1994 became mostly famous for the reluctance of the international community to intervene. France's late intervention towards the end of the crisis is dealt with here purely from a French point of view. The actual non-intervention case from a US American point of view will be dealt with later on in this study.

70 Bellamy (2004) Op. Cit. 219 (p. 138).

71 Kuperman (2000) (p. 98).

72 Ibid (p.96).

73 Magnarella (2005) (p. 816).

had lost its urgency.[74] At the time of intervention, both French President Francois Mitterrand and his government failed to properly address the humanitarian crisis as a severe genocide. Despite overwhelming evidence of the severity of the killings, Mitterrand only declared on May 16th 1994 in an appearance on French TF1 that the situation in Rwanda was genocide.[75] Nonetheless, the public reference to the crisis and the suffering of individuals suggests that Mitterrand's decision was at least partially driven by the motivation to save the endangered population on the ground. The altruistic character of this motivation, however, is highly doubtful, bearing in mind French entanglement in the crisis.[76]

Public Awareness and Media Coverage [0,5]

From the beginning of the genocide in April 1994, French media took the lead in Europe in misinforming the public and diverting the focus away from the actual massacres to the suffering of refugees in neighbouring countries. The extent of the suffering on the ground was either played down or not made visible by the media. Coverage was minimal throughout the first half of 1994. Instead, the French media characterized the conflict as a sort of civil war that originated in the injustices of colonial times, disregarding the fact that the conflict evolved into genocide between two unequal parties.[77] Consequently, Gouteaux (2008) claims that the French media failed to induce a sense of urgency to the French public or even to alarm the French government to do something about the humanitarian catastrophe on the ground.[78] That is to say, that the media only reported hesitantly about the situation on ground and thereby failed to create a public awareness that might have pressured the government to intervene for the sake of saving suffering civilians.

Feeling of moral obligation to intervene by the decision-maker [0]

Due to the fact that the French state had widely supported the francophone regime of Habyarimana during the civil war and afterwards through financial aid, arms deals and even the training of troops, President Mitterrand as the main decision maker to intervene felt a sense of moral obligation to intervene and bring the genocide to an end.[79] This feeling of moral obligation, however, most likely did not root in truly altruistic sentiments but rather derives from feelings of guilt and partial responsibility for the catastrophe. Hence, this feeling of moral obligation to intervene cannot be described as altruistic and does therefore not trigger a deflection on the altruism scale.

---

[74] Wheeler and Bellamy (2008) Op. Cit. 44 (p. 533).

[75] CEC (2004).

[76] See *Feeling of moral obligation to intervene by the decision-maker* (following page).

[77] Jaboeuf (2008).

[78] Ibid.

[79] McQueen (2006) Op. Cit. 47 (p. 143).

Economic Interest [0]

Since "[...] Rwanda is a poor rural country with about 90 % of the population engaged in (mainly subsistence) agriculture [...] and with few natural resources and minimal industry [...]",[80] the country in contrary to other Central African countries has never been of any economic interests to Western states. Therefore, it is highly doubtful that France had economic interests at stake in Rwanda.

Geo-Strategic Interest [5]

France's policy in Africa and particularly in regards to Habyarimana's Hutu regime in Kigali has been strongly influenced by post-colonial geo-strategic interests in the regions. The degree of national interests involved in the intervention in Rwanda was perceived to be that high that experts have regarded French intervention to be an abuse of the principle of humanitarian intervention.[81] Under President Mitterrand, France was trying to buy credibility as a *grand nation* in Africa. After the end of the Cold War several francophone nations were looking for new donor states and Mitterrand feared that losing one protégé with Rwanda might set in motion a domino effect that might trigger further states to turn their back on French influence.[82] The break away of Soviet influence in Africa had facilitated the spread of Anglo-American interests threatening French interests in the region. The Ugandan based Tutsi RPF [83] that had been fighting Habyarimana's Hutu regime throughout the civil war invaded Rwanda from the North as soon as the genocide began. Evidence suggests that France feared that a victory by the Anglophone RPF could result in a consolidation of British or American influence in Rwanda at the expense of France.[84] Thus, intervention can be understood as a means to stop the advance of the approaching RPF and retain control of Rwandan affairs—a behaviour that has been named Fashoda syndrome, namely a tendency within French foreign policy from colonial times to secure French influence in regions that have become vulnerable to British influence.[85] That way Operation Turquoise can be understood as a continuation of the supportive policy of the Hutu regime in Kigali by other means.

Political Interest of the Decision Maker [2,5]

France's approach to Habyarimana's regime and the later decision to intervene was to a great extent shaped by Mitterrand's personal preferences. Mitterrand who had gained the name *l'Afrique* for his personal dedication to Africa and decolonization policy managed to escape normal checks and balances from the cabinet and developed personal relations with most of the francophone African leaders.

---

80 CIA (2010).

81 Wheeler and Bellamy (2008) Op. Cit. 44 (p. 532).

82 McQueen (2006) Op. Cit. 47 (p. 130).

83 RPF = Rwandan People's Front.

84 Klinghoffer (1998).

85 McQueen (2006) Op. Cit. 47(p. 132).

Habyarimana's family were personal friends of the Mitterrands and the cause of the Hutus was a matter of personal concern for Mitterrand.[86] Further, Mitterrand was driven by political considerations and concern about his own place in history. "[...] He did not want to be remembered as the president who fiddled while Rwanda burned [...]".[87] Hence, one can state that the decision to intervene at last was a decision that served both the political and personal interests of French President Mitterrand.

Despite the altruistic component of the motivation to conduct Operation *Turquoise* by the French government in 1994, the intervention was hardly altruistic overall. The main factors triggering French intervention were of geo-strategic and political nature. If Mitterrand or his government were actually driven by altruistic sentiments, intervention would have taken place at an earlier stage. The reason for France's late initiative was that the francophone Hutu movement was about to lose ground against an approaching anglophone RPF.

3.2.5 Bosnia (Operation **Deliberate Force,** *1995)*

After the independence of Slovenia and Croatia in 1991, also the Bosnians were striving for independence from Belgrade. When Bosnian Serbs proclaimed the State of Bosnia and Herzegovina, the Bosnian Muslims brought forward a referendum that was supposed to bring about a solution for Bosnia's future. Due to the fact that only Muslim Bosnians participated in the referendum the result was 99.4 % in favour of independence. On March 3rd 1993 the President of Bosnia and Herzegovina, Izetbegovic, declared Bosnia's independence from Belgrade. The main leader of the Bosnian Serbs Karadzic, however, declared loyalty to Serbia while his militias backed up by the government in Belgrade began to seize towns and villages in Eastern Bosnia in early April 1993. Initially the international community reacted by delivering humanitarian aid without actively intervening to stop the emerging violence. The UN concentrated on creating safe havens around strategic locations in order for the displaced civilian population to seek refuge from the belligerent parties. Throughout 1993 and 1994 the international community was careful not to jeopardize the lives of the UN soldiers on the ground by reacting decisively to the mounting Serbian aggression against UN personnel and civilians in the UN supervised safe havens. After witnessing the massacre of Srebrenica and the continuous mortar shelling of civilians in Sarajevo, the NATO leadership decided in August 1995 to react to Serbian aggression with an airpower campaign.[88] Since the decision to intervene was a collective decision by all NATO

---

[86] Ibid (p. 134).

[87] Jakobsen (1996) Op. Cit. 224.

[88] McQueen (2006) Op. Cit. 47 (pp. 55–80).

member states I will focus on NATO's motivation as an institution as well as its member state's motivation to use force in Bosnia.

Existence of an acute humanitarian crisis [4]

After almost three years of continuous fighting Bosnia had turned into a war zone where civilians were deliberately targeted by the belligerent parties. Ethnic cleansing, displacement, constant targeting through artillery and snipers, starvation and murder had increased the number of all victims in Bosnia to more than a million by 1995.[89] Individual instances of war crimes committed against civilians such as the massacre of Srebrenica killing more than 6,000 men or the ongoing mortar shelling of civilians in besieged Sarajevo raised allegations of genocide and caused the international community to set up an international criminal tribunal to prosecute war criminals.[90] The high number of casualties and the severity of atrocities committed caused the situation on the ground in Bosnia to become a supreme humanitarian emergency, i.e. a humanitarian crisis that had to be brought to an end in order to avoid more innocent people getting killed.[91] The severity of humanitarian crisis triggered the leaders of NATO member states to strongly address the crisis on the ground in Bosnia and to make the humanitarian motive the prime justification for intervention. Clinton stated explicitly in an interview with the *New York Times* that "[...] we [US] clearly have a humanitarian interest in helping to prevent the strangulation of Sarajevo and the continuing slaughter of innocents in Bosnia [...]".[92] In a press conference immediately after the end of Operation Deliberate Force in September 1995 Clinton asserted again that strikes have been carried out "[...] to prevent further slaughter of innocent civilians in the Sarajevo area and in the other safe areas of Bosnia [...]".[93] Also the Foreign Minister of Germany Kinkel stated that NATO's airpower campaign primarily intended to ensure that Sarajevo could breathe freely again.[94] Hence, it is fair to state that the brutality of the atrocities committed and the explicit condemnation of the crisis by NATO leaders can be valued as an indicator for an at least partially altruistic motivation.

Public Awareness and Media Coverage [3]

Due to the fact that the disintegration of Yugoslavia took place in the backyard of NATO's heartland, the media covered the conflict from the beginning in the 1990s. In particular the crisis in Bosnia and the deterioration of the humanitarian conditions on the ground over the years became a major focus of Western media. From 1992 until the actual intervention in 1995 the coverage of Bosnia dominated the

---

[89] Ryter (2003) Op. Cit. 17 (p. 39).

[90] Sklenka, S.D. Op. Cit. 155 (p. 12).

[91] Owen (2001) (p. 66).

[92] Jehl (1994a).

[93] Clinton (1995).

[94] Höges (1995) (p. 22).

headlines more than any other crisis during that time, both in the US and Western Europe.[95] While the media coverage of the crisis in Bosnia initially remained unbiased, presenting the crisis as a civil war or ethnic conflict, the increasing portrayal of the Serbs as the aggressors predominately by German Chancellor Kohl and French President Mitterrand changed the tone of the Western media towards the conflict.[96] Witnessing the atrocities committed by Serbian militias against Bosniak civilians the Western media began quoting Western politicians characterizing the Serbs as "[...] illiterates, degenerates, baby killers and rapists [...]".[97] The anti-Serbian tendencies together with graphic images of the suffering civilians on the ground created a sense of urgency in Western public opinion to do something. The antagonistic image presented of the Bosnian Serbs and the regime in Belgrade by the media, aroused public opinion in Europe and in the US to become increasingly hostile towards the Serbs. Consequently, Western governments felt mounting public pressure in 1995 particularly after the massacres of Srebrenica to do something to stop the suffering of civilians.[98]

Feeling of moral obligation to intervene by the decision-maker [0]

In his autobiography Clinton stated in 2004 that "[...] as television and print media finally brought the horror of a Serb-run detention camp in northern Bosnia home to Europeans and Americans, I spoke out in favor of NATO air strikes with U.S. involvement [...]".[99] Clinton's statement gives the impression as if his decision in favour of air strikes was directly connected to being exposed to the graphic pictures presented in the media. However, it remains questionable to what extent Clinton's personal compassionate feelings drove the decision of the US and NATO to intervene. The fact that no other leader of a NATO member state explicitly expressed his personal concern for the fate of the civilian population prior to the intervention in 1995 suggests that personal feelings of altruism in the political leaderships of NATO member states were greatly absent.

Economic Interest [1,5]

The disintegration of the Eastern Bloc had revealed lucrative market opportunities for many Western European companies, particularly German companies, in Central and Eastern Europe who were eager to capitalize on the arising liberal market economies. By 1992, Germany was the single most important trading partner for most countries in Eastern Europe and the Balkans, including Yugoslavia.[100] Companies such as Hoechst, Volkswagen or Siemens were strongly committed to their investments in the Balkans and wanted to ensure that these

95 Robinson (2001) Op. Cit. 249 (p. 954).

96 Lucarelli (2000) (p. 34).

97 Cohn (2003) (p. 122).

98 Murray-Miller (2007) (p. 11).

99 Clinton (2004) (p. 464).

100 Murray-Miller (2007) Op. Cit. 316 (p. 9).

investments were not to be jeopardized by an ongoing crisis.[101] While Croatia and Slovenia had long been lucrative outlets for German industrial goods, Serbia and Bosnia offered promising opportunities for German companies to expand their economic sphere of influence. Apart from German companies, also other Western European and American companies had great interests at stake in the Balkans.[102] Thus, the economic interests in the Balkans as a lucrative outlet and cost-efficient production site most likely facilitated the decision of several NATO member states to finally bring stability to Bosnia.

Geo-Strategic Interest [4]

The conflict in Bosnia was raging in the backyard of Western Europe and constituted to be a potential security threat to the neighbouring countries. Afraid of a spill over, NATO was motivated in its intervention by "[...] the importance of preventing a wider war in Europe [...]".[103] Not only for the new nation states in Eastern Europe but also for the states of 'old Europe', the reality of millions of displaced individuals trying to enter Western Europe posed a major security threat. As Clinton outlined in 1994 "[...] We have an interest in stemming the destabilizing flows of refugees that this horrible conflict is creating [...]".[104] Particularly Germany faced an inflow of more than 220,000 refugees from Bosnia that were to remain in the FRG so long as the conflict was not resolved. Up until the end of the 1990s a considerable amount of refugees remained in Germany having a hard time integrating into German society. Therefore, above all Germany had a particular interest in resolving the conflict in order to allow for the refugees to return home.[105] Apart from these more obvious security concerns arising from the "[...] first difficult security crisis in Europe after the Cold War [...]",[106] NATO as an institution had specific interests at hand in intervening in the crisis in Bosnia as well. With the disappearance of the perceived Communist peril coming from Central and Eastern Europe, NATO saw itself obligated to redefine its role from a defence alliance into a proactive military institution promoting neo-liberal values in struggling democracies and proliferating Western security interests.[107] It has been claimed that particularly the US, as the only remaining superpower, tried to take the opportunity to replace Soviet influence in Eurasia in order to consolidate American hegemony in the region.[108] Clinton explicitly stated in 1994 that "[...] We [the US] have an interest in showing that NATO, history's greatest military

---

101 Ash (1994) (p. 403).

102 Redburn (1993).

103 Jehl (1994) Op. Cit. 310.

104 Cited in Ibid.

105 Cox (1998) (p. 618).

106 Clinton (2004) Op. Cit. 311.

107 Murray-Miller (2007) (Op. Cit. 316 (p. 14).

108 Ibid (p. 15).

alliance, remains a credible force for peace in post-cold-war Europe [...]",[109] thereby suggesting that NATO decision making might have been to a great extent driven by US interests to bolster NATO's standing in the region.

Political Interest of the Decision Maker [2,5]

Due to media coverage and public awareness of the atrocities, Western politicians were greatly motivated to authorize an intervention to gain electoral popularity. Moreover, US President Clinton apparently realized in 1995, a year before presidential elections, that it was time to settle the conflict within his first term. Having criticized Bush during campaigning in 1992 for not having done enough in Bosnia, "[...] Clinton seems to have decided, rather suddenly, that the Bosnian war should be settled before next year's American presidential elections [...]"[110] so as not to lose his credibility *vis-à-vis* his electorate. Thus, at least the decision of the US to mobilize NATO to intervene in Bosnia in 1995 was driven by Clinton's political interests in improving his image a year before presidential elections.

NATO's decision to respond to Serbia's aggression in Bosnia in 1995 with Operation *Deliberate Force* was equally motivated by altruistic and self-interested factors. NATO's geo-strategic interests in the region as well as the existence of an acute and severe humanitarian crisis were the most important factors that triggered NATO to coercively intervene in Bosnia after almost three years of passivity. The fear of a protracted conflict so close to the Western European heartland that could not be solved anymore by diplomatic means was probably the single most important national interest-based motivation for most NATO member states to agree to air strikes.

3.2.6 Kosovo (Operation **Allied Force**, *1999)*

Kosovo, an autonomous province of Yugoslavia until 1989, had been widely forgotten over the wars of separation of other provinces throughout the 1990s. With other former Yugoslav provinces breaking up from the rule in Belgrade and increasing Serb suppression of Albanian cultural activities the predominately Muslim Kosovo Albanians were striving for independence from Serbia. In 1996 a rebel insurgency group, called the Kosovo Liberation Army (KLA) made up of young Marxist-Leninists and frustrated Albanian Kosovar nationalists, emerged, launching attacks against Serb administrative offices and police stations.[111] Milosevic's government in Belgrade responded harshly against these attacks by killing Kosovar civilians that were alleged of having supported or participated in the KLA. With the situation about to escalate the UN Security Council issued UN

[109] Jehl (1994b) Op. Cit. 310.

[110] The Economist (1995).

[111] Shugarman (2006) (p. 4).

SC Resolution 1199 (1998) "[…] Affirming that the deterioration of the situation in Kosovo […] constitutes a threat to peace and security in the region […]"[112] putting pressure on the Serbian government to improve the humanitarian situation in the region.[113] After failing to solve the crisis diplomatically with a proposed Peace Plan in Paris in March 1999, NATO decided to intervene militarily with Operation Allied Force on March 24th, 1999 against the will of Russia and China, thereby without the consent of the UN Security Council. Due to the fact that the decision to intervene was a collective decision by NATO member states this book will focus upon the motivation to intervene by NATO as an institution and its most important member states.

Existence of an acute humanitarian crisis [3]

Despite the fact that Western politicians tried to create the impression as if Serbian activities in Kosovo in the beginning of 1999 were about to cause another Holocaust,[114] the humanitarian crisis at hand was a moderately severe crisis in comparison to the humanitarian situation after the intervention of NATO. Nonetheless, the humanitarian crisis was acute and had to be brought to a halt since until intervention in March 1999 approximately 230,000 people were displaced and more than 10,000 were killed in massacres all over the region.[115] Initial UN estimates reporting about more than 44,000 casualties turned out to be inaccurate. Receiving reports about massacres throughout Kosovo, large scale ethnic cleansing on the way and the aggressive Serbian reputation the international community had to be aware that the situation was alarming. The humanitarian crisis was determinedly addressed by all NATO leaders and the cessation of this crisis was stated to be the sole intention and motivation for NATO to intervene. In his Chicago Speech UK Prime Minister Tony Blair declared that "[…] We cannot let the evil of ethnic cleansing stand […]" and that the objective of NATO was to bring about "[…] a verifiable cessation of all combat activities and killings […]".[116] In the same way also President Clinton addressed the humanitarian crisis in Kosovo stating after outlining the extent of atrocities committed that "[…] Kosovo's crisis now is full-blown, and if we do not act, clearly, it will get even worse […]".[117] Thus, even though the humanitarian crisis was not as severe as presumed prior to the intervention, it was nonetheless sufficiently acute so as to constitute a severe humanitarian crisis. The public reference by all NATO leaders to the crisis serves as an indicator for an at least partially altruistic motivation.

---

112 UN Security Council (1998).

113 Ryter (2003) Op. Cit. 17 (p. 44).

114 Ibid (p. 13).

115 Bjorna (2009) Op. Cit. 38 (p. 96).

116 Blair (1999).

117 Clinton (1999).

Public Awareness and Media Coverage [1,5]

The media attention surrounding the humanitarian and political crisis in the Southern province of Yugoslavia was strong. The atrocities committed by the Serbs were one of the leading news stories in the beginning of 1999 triggering public awareness and support for military intervention.[118] Similar to the conflict in Bosnia four years earlier media and public attention were incited by reports and information distributed by the governments of NATO member states. In particular the German and the American government relied upon reports, which some claimed were actually fabricated, that presented the Serbs as aggressors committing war crimes leading up to genocide.[119] Western governments constructed a demonized image of the Serbs based on evidence of massacres committed by Serb forces against Kosovar civilians as well as based on the entire Operation Horseshoe, an alleged plan of Yugoslav forces to expel Kosovars from Kosovo. Without questioning the integrity of the information flow during the war the Western media relied upon these reports while developing an anti-Serb rhetoric that dominated the headlines for months particularly in Germany and the US.[120] In spite of the actual acts of aggression and human rights abuses committed by Serbian authorities, the image created by the Western media was presenting the Serbs as unilaterally responsible for the crisis. Fuelled by the memories of Serb atrocities in Bosnia, some news reports were speaking about a new Holocaust happening in Kosovo.[121] Since public pressure was induced by Western political leaderships, its ability to trigger NATO member states to adopt a rather altruistic decision is questionable. Thus, media and public attention does not really serve as an accurate indictor of an altruistic motivation underlying the decision to intervene in Kosovo.

Feeling of moral obligation to intervene by the decision-maker [0]

Evidence for any particular personal feelings of moral obligation to intervene among NATO decision makers could not be found.

Economic Interest [0]

Kosovo was traditionally the poorest region in Yugoslavia and was of little economic significance for any NATO member state.[122]

Geo-Strategic Interest [4,5]

The crisis in Kosovo once again took place in close proximity to NATO and EU member states making the cessation of hostilities an issue of a particular security interest. Apart from the altruistic motivation to intervene on basis of humanitarian grounds, NATO as a whole and the US in particular, were driven by two main

---

118 Domagala (2004) Op. Cit. 18 (p. 25).

119 Wolfgram (2008) (p. 1).

120 Ibid (p. 12).

121 Ryter (2003) Op. Cit. 17 (p. 13).

122 Bjorna (2009) Op. Cit. 38 (p. 97).

strategic and security interests: consolidating long-lasting peace and security in Europe as well as ensuring that NATO as an institution could maintain its credibility as an effective military alliance capable of enforcing its interests if necessary.[123] The security interest of NATO and Western governments was primarily incited by the refugee streams of hundreds of thousands of Kosovo Albanians moving towards neighbouring countries, particularly Macedonia, Albania and Bulgaria threatening the stability on the Balkans.[124] Further, NATO was eager to finally bring about a regime change in Belgrade since Milosevic's repeated attempts to expand or consolidate Serbian influence in the Balkans were a source of instability in a region close to the European heartland.[125] Following NATO intervention, Milosevic was indicted on May 27 1999 for war crimes and crimes against humanity, the first step towards the downfall of his regime.[126] Secondly, NATO under the leadership of the US had particular interests in presenting itself as a guarantor of peace and stability beyond Western Europe. The crisis in Bosnia had left NATO behind as a weak alliance that had presented itself as irresolute and incredible. The crisis in Kosovo offered the opportunity to repair NATO's tattered reputation and to regain credibility as a powerful peace enforcement alliance.[127] This particular strategic interest of NATO as an institution was outlined by Blair in his Chicago Speech where he stated that

> "[...] *On its 50th birthday NATO must prevail. Milosevic had, I believe, convinced himself that the Alliance would crack. But I am certain that this weekend's Summit in Washington under President Clinton's leadership will make our unity and our absolute resolve clear for all to see* [...]".[128]

Thus, it seems fairly obvious that the geo-strategic interests of NATO and its member states were the main driving force to intervene in Kosovo.

Political Interest of the Decision Maker [1]

Even though the intervention in Kosovo was not used by the main decision makers in NATO to boost their political standing before an election, at least in the case of President Clinton it seems plausible that the intervention in Kosovo was used to divert public attention away from the Lewinsky scandal and the subsequent impeachment.[129] The Lewinsky-scandal in the beginning of 1998 and in particular the failed impeachment of President Clinton towards the end of 1998 had aroused public opinion. Just a few months before the intervention in Kosovo the entire scandal and its aftermath had seriously tarnished his image.[130] The intervention in

---

123 Wheeler (2002) Op. Cit. 54 (p. 265).

124 Bellamy (2002) (p. 3).

125 Gleddisch et al. (1997) Op. Cit. 278(p. 15).

126 Scharf (1999).

127 Krauthammer (1985) Op. Cit. 173 (p. 1).

128 Blair (1999) Op. Cit. 334.

129 Schlafley (1999).

130 Williams and Delli Carpini (2000) (p. 68).

Kosovo was an attempt to repair Clinton's image and divert media and public attention away from negative sentiments in the American public in regards to his person in 1998.

Operation *Allied Force* in Kosovo was motivated almost to an equal extent by altruism and national/self-interest. The main factor driving NATO member states to intervene was the presence of strong geo-strategic interests.

3.2.7 East Timor (Operation Stabilise*/INTERFET, 1999)*

The financial crisis in South-East Asia 1997 struck Indonesia intensively and the resulting economic collapse caused a social collapse that triggered periodic outbursts of violence against the regime in the country. In particular in regions where minorities were dominant, like in East Timor, opposition against the government was growing. The continuous quest for independence by a majority of East Timorese since the annexation of the eastern part of the island by Indonesia in 1975 had paved the way for a UN supervised referendum on 30 August 1999 in which the East Timorese could decide their future. Despite the fact that a great majority, 78.5 %, of the voters opted for independence, violence broke out between pro-and anti-independence groups immediately after the announcement of the result. With the Indonesian army involved in the hostilities a quick solution of the crisis domestically appeared to be unrealistic.[131] Responding to the occurring humanitarian crisis the UN Security Council adopted Resolution 1264 (1999) authorizing an international intervention force under the leadership of Australia to take all necessary measures "[…] to restore peace and security in East Timor […]".[132] On September 9th 1999 Australian forces belonging to Operation Spitfire landed at Dili Airport as the spearhead of Operation Stabilise. Due to the fact that Australia provided the biggest intervention force as well as planned the operations, this book will focus on the decision making of Australia.

Existence of an acute humanitarian crisis [4]

UN Security Council Resolution 1264 (1999) justified intervention based on the "[…] continuing violence against and large-scale displacement and relocation of East Timorese civilians […]"[133] following the ballot. Indeed, the humanitarian crisis at hand was acute. After the announcement of the results of the referendum the Indonesian military began a mission of forced displacement driving more than 250,000 civilians over the border to Western Timor.[134] According to the Indonesian Commission of Investigation into Human Rights Violations more than

---

[131] Nayaran (2000) (p. 97).

[132] UN Security Council (1999).

[133] Ibid.

[134] Fernandes (2008) (p. 93).

70 % of the buildings in East Timor were destroyed, vital infrastructure was demolished and entire cities were left without access to running water or electricity.[135] In addition to the fact that a quarter of the entire population was displaced, over 1,000 lives had been lost in a matter of days making the humanitarian crisis acute as officials feared genocide against the East Timorese was imminent.[136] In face of this supreme humanitarian emergency the Australian government under the leadership of Prime Minister Howard did not shy away from condemning the violence and declaring that the intervention is motivated by the aim to bring the human suffering to an end. In his address to the nation on September 19th 1999 Howard declared that "[…] We have all sensed that a small, vulnerable community was about to be denied the freedom they have sought for so long and voted so overwhelmingly to achieve […]" and that after having witnessed "[…] scenes of violence, death and destruction in East Timor […]" Australia had to act to restore peace and stability.[137] Hence, it is fair to say that Australia's decision to intervene was to a great extent driven by the feeling of urgency to end this humanitarian crisis.

Public Awareness and Media Coverage [4,5]

The crisis in East Timor created massive media attention portraying the full extent of atrocities committed and calling for an immediate stop of violence.

> […] *The violence following the referendum became front-page news in every Australian newspaper, and television pictures of the atrocities galvanized the Australian public into demanding action to end the violence* […].[138]

Thus, the East Timor crisis constitutes a classic CNN effect where graphic and expressive media coverage incites the public to call on the government to do something to halt the violence. Already prior to the crisis in 1999 public opinion in Australia was compassionate with the fate of the East Timorese and their struggle for independence. The injustice of the annexation of East Timor by Indonesia in 1975 and the Australian government's silence over the atrocities committed against the civilian population was still well-remembered by most Australians. Civil society groups that had emerged over the decades prompted a policy shift in Australia prioritizing a solution of the East Timorese question over a pro-Indonesian Jakarta-first policy. With the occurring violence and the obvious involvement of the Indonesian army, the pressure of the Australian public to do something became that strong that it could no longer be ignored by the government.[139] In particular the feeling of having betrayed East Timor's right for independence for decades was a decisive factor for the Australian public to pressure the government

135 KPP HAM (2002) (Ch. II p. 6ff).

136 Wheeler and Dunne (2001) (p. 816).

137 Howard (1999).

138 Wheeler and Dunne (2001) Op. Cit 354 (p. 817).

139 Fernandes (2008) Op. Cit. 352 (p. 97).

to take an altruistic decision in order to save the lives of thousands of suffering East Timorese.[140]

Feeling of moral obligation to intervene by the decision-maker [0]

Unlike his predecessors Prime Minister Howard "[...] saw himself as less ideologically motivated in relation to foreign policy [...]"[141] and was commonly believed to be rather pragmatic than ethically or morally stirred. Howard's reliance on rational interest-based motivation suggests that he would not let his decision making be impacted by any personal feelings of moral obligation to intervene.

Economic Interest [2,5]

Due to the geographic proximity of Indonesia and East Timor to the Australian mainland trade between the two regions has always been mutually beneficial. Domestic violence and instability in East Timor or other regions of Indonesia certainly raised trade concerns in Australia for which the archipelago is an important outlet for Australian exports. Thus, it was in the interest of the Australian economy to bring peace and security to Timor and Indonesia.[142] Moreover, Australia was certainly interested in the continuous profitable access to the lucrative resources of the Timor Gap. Following intervention in 1999 Australia and UNTAET [143] agreed on a Joint Petroleum Development Area dividing up East Timor's petroleum production between East Timor (90 %) and Australia (10 %). In fact, Australia is granted control of 82 % of the largest oil field in the Timor Gap, Greater Sunrise, which transfers two billion BOE of oil to the Australian market, resulting in a 59 % loss of petroleum revenue for East Timor annually.[144] Thus, by intervening in East Timor Australia seized the opportunity to receive privileged access to lucrative oil fields as well as ensured the internal stability of an important export market.

Geo-Strategic Interest [3,5]

Howard's Coalition government had particular geo-strategic interests at stake in the security and stability in the region of South East Asia. Evolving from the moralist foreign policy outlooks of his predecessors Prime Minister Howard approached the crisis in East Timor from the standpoint of regionalism, i.e. suggesting that Australia should get involved in a conflict that was so close to its own territory.[145] In Australia's Strategic Policy 1997 issued by the Ministry of Defence the importance of regional security and stability was outlined as follows:

---

140 Wheeler and Dunne (2001) Op. Cit. 354 (p. 817).

141 McDougall (2002) (p. 8).

142 Wheeler and Dunne (2001) Op. Cit. 354 (p. 809).

143 UNTAET = United Nations Transitional Administration in East Timor .

144 Ahmed (2006) (p. 228).

145 McDougall (2002) Op. Cit. 359 (p. 9).

"[...] *Australia's strategic interests do not begin and end at our shoreline. It would be a serious mistake to think we could adopt a 'fortress Australia' strategy in the event of a deterioration of regional stability. We cannot be secure in an insecure region* [...]".[146]

With an ethnic conflict such as the conflict in East Timor having the potential to severely destabilize a neighbouring country such as Indonesia, Australia had to be concerned about its own security. The White Paper 'In the National Interest', published in 1997, explicitly mentions the strategic importance of Asia Pacific for Australia by stating that "[...] Australia's most important strategic and economic interests lie in a region—the Asia Pacific [...]".[147] Hence, by taking over a leading role in securing peace and stability in this region Australia was certainly advancing its own geo-strategic interests as one of the main regional powers.

Political Interest of the Decision Maker [1]

Due to the fact that public outrage in Australia reached tsunami-like proportions when the media began to cover the atrocities it was within the political interest of the Howard administration to satisfy the electorate by intervening in East Timor to end the violence.[148]

The Australian humanitarian intervention in East Timor presents a case of an even motivation that was comprised almost equally by altruism and national/self-interest. While the Australian public pushed for an intervention to save the lives of the East-Timorese, Prime Minister Howard and his government were more interested in securing vital economic and geo-strategic interests. Overall, the intervention was slightly more self-interested than altruistic.

3.2.8 Sierra Leone (Operation **Palliser**, *2000)*

After several *coup d'états* throughout the 1990s Sierra Leone experienced a period of political instability, organised violence and economic exploitation. Particularly the growing influence of the Revolutionary United Front (RUF) throughout the country and their control over arms and diamond trade had severely destabilized Sierra Leone and neighbouring countries. Two peacekeeping forces, ECOWAS and UNAMSIL, attempted between 1997 and 2000 to restore peace and stability in a country that had been defined by lawlessness and failed governance.[149] In a repeated attack on UNAMSIL forces in May 2000 RUF managed to seize several armed carriers and threatened to march on the capital Freetown to regain power. As a response UN Secretary General Annan called on the international community and particularly Britain as the former colonial power to intervene to save

146 McLachlan (1997) (p. 3).

147 Dept. of Foreign Affairs and Trade. (1997).

148 Fernandes (2008) Op. Cit. 352 (p. 93).

149 Vesel (2004) (p. 24).

UNAMSIL from collapse.[150] Both UN SC Resolution 1289 (2000) and 1299 (2000) addressed the crisis in Sierra Leone and stated "[…] that that the situation in Sierra Leone continues to constitute a threat to international peace and security in the region […]"[151] without explicitly authorizing intervention. On May 8th, 2000, after a request by the British High Commissioner in Freetown to evacuate British citizens before the RUF reached the city centre, British forces landed in Freetown. In this book I will analyse the decision making process of the British government to intervene.

Existence of an acute humanitarian crisis [2,5]

Since the first attacks by the RUF on Sierra Leonean territory in 1991 the rebel organization has been strongly committed to consolidate its influence over the resource abundant regions in Eastern Sierra Leone mainly by terrorizing the civilian population. In absence of proper governance, the RUF used mutilation, rape and child abduction as means to establish their dominance.[152] This widespread indiscriminate violence caused between 20,000 and 50,000 deads over the years while leaving more than 30,000 individuals mutilated and more than 250,000 women raped.[153] Having remained inactive over the years leading up to the intervention in 2000, Britain decided to intervene when the humanitarian crisis had lost most of its urgency. With the RUF marching on Freetown once again the humanitarian situation on the ground was threatened once more. To state however, that the humanitarian situation in May 2000 was as supreme as other humanitarian crisis presented in this book would be exaggerated.[154] Yet, Prime Minister Blair addressed this medium scale humanitarian crisis in a public statement on May 19, 2000 by stating that

> "[…] *It is an appalling savagery inflicted upon the civilian population in which rape and slavery and mutilation are the everyday weapons. It's a campaign of butchery in which* […] *young children have had their arms and their legs hacked off as a warning to others* […]".[155]

Fearing that the RUF could once again terrorize the capital, Blair declares that he authorized intervention to stop the advancing rebels and secure the lives of British citizens. Hence, among other motivations, the humanitarian motive certainly played a role in intervening in Sierra Leone as to avert an ever more severe humanitarian crisis to come.[156]

[150] Woods and Reese (2008) (p. 60).

[151] UN Security Council (2000)

[152] Ibid (p.31).

[153] Ploughshares (2002).

[154] Bellamy and Williams (2005) (p. 184).

[155] Blair (2000).

[156] Bellamy and Williams (2005) Op. Cit. 372 (p. 180).

Public Awareness and Media Coverage [1]

Despite the obvious atrocities committed by RUF against the civilian population the conflict in Sierra Leone did not attract great media attention in Britain like the conflicts on the Balkans or in Northern Ireland at the time. While the media mainly focused on a political scandal surrounding the British government's involvement in delivering extensive arms shipments to President Kabbah despite supporting a UN arms embargo for Sierra Leone, the media coverage of the human suffering on the ground however, was minimal at best.[157] In fact, British media was even relatively sceptical about the severity of crisis at hand and the need for British involvement.[158] Even though the public responded with harsh criticism to the British violation of its own arms embargo, there was little public awareness of the crisis on the ground.[159] In actual fact, the British public took even a highly critical standpoint towards Blair's decision to intervene as the public feared another 'Black-Hawk Down' type involvement in just another African civil war in times where the British military faced an overstretch already. With the engagement in Bosnia and Kosovo, British public opinion did not see the necessity for the British military to get involved in another crisis far away from home.[160] Hence, while the British public, not fully aware of the humanitarian crisis, did not call for an intervention to save lives, British media only hesitantly reported about the crisis and might have had a minimal impact on the altruism involved in the decision to intervene.

Feeling of moral obligation to intervene by the decision-maker [2]

Tony Blair, as an outspoken advocate of basing political decision on morals had envisaged a new approach to foreign policy on basis of a "[...] doctrine of international community [...] a community based on the equal worth of all, on the foundation of mutual rights and mutual responsibility [...]".[161] In particular towards Africa Blair formulated his 'ethical foreign policy' to promote values in order to foster a new partnership between the West and Africa. "His decision to take action in Sierra Leone can be traced to his so-called "ethical foreign policy" and even deeper to his personal values [...]".[162] Thus, Blair's feeling of moral obligation to intervene might have made up a great share of the motivation to do something.

Economic Interest [1,5]

Sierra Leone's most lucrative and internationally most wanted resource, diamonds, have fuelled the conflict and certainly had some impact on Britain's decision to intervene. With an annual market value of 4.2 billion GBP, producing jewellery

157 Shah (2001).

158 Bellamy and Williams (2005) Op. Cit. 372(p. 180).

159 Kampfner (2003) (p. 67).

160 Evoe (2008) (p. 67).

161 Kampfner (2003) Op. Cit. 377 (p. 75).

162 Evoe (2008) Op. Cit. 378 (p. 88).

worth 35 billion GBP, the diamond trade has become Sierra Leone's most profitable economic activity raising economic interests abroad.[163] According to Pilger (2000) British and Americans multinationals were meeting representatives of the Sierra Leonean government and RUF rebel leaders in charge of diamond mining in March 2000 negotiating about a deal to ensure Western access to the RUF diamond mines. After having been repulsed by the RUF and fearing the break away of business and jobs in the UK, Britain intervened allegedly driven by the motivation to secure the control over the precious resource.[164]

Geo-Strategic Interest [4]

The prime motivator for the British government to deploy soldiers around the capital Freetown was the fact that British citizens were at risk due to the advancing RUF forces. As Blair outlined in his public statement "[…] The main task for the British forces was to help evacuate safely the hundreds of British citizens who risked being trapped in Sierra Leone […]".[165] Operation Palliser was initially planned to be a traditional rescue and evacuation mission without drawing British soldiers into the role of direct combatants.[166] The actual military objective to secure greater parts of Sierra Leone was only introduced as the Quick Reaction Force was already on its way. However, Blair's administration had a particular interest in supporting the erection of a democratic regime in Sierra Leone by avoiding the RUF as a band of anarchists to gain political power again. "[…] Britain has a national interest in the promotion of our values […] and must support the demands of other peoples for the democratic, rights on which we insist for ourselves […]"[167] Blair declared on a press conference in 1997. Ensuring regional stability within Western Africa by promoting a democratically elected government in Freetown can be understood a way for Britain to advance its strategic national interests. With the RUF extending its reign of influence the democratically elected government's ability to govern was seriously undermined. Hence, one of Britain's motivations to intervene was to secure regional stability in one of its former colonies.[168]

Political Interest of the Decision Maker [2]

The crisis in Sierra Leone provided Blair with the opportunity to repair his domestic image that had been tarnished by both his late response to the humanitarian crisis after the flood in Mozambique earlier in 2000 and the Blair administration's

[163] Pilger (2000).

[164] Pilger (2000).

[165] Blair (1999) Op.Cit. 373.

[166] Evoe (2008) Op. Cit. 378 (p. 2).

[167] Coates and Krieger (2004) (p. 16).

[168] Roberson (2007) (p. 19).

responsibility for an arm shipment around the arms embargo to Sierra Leone.[169] Showing resolve to support the democratic regime in Freetown and the UN mission in Sierra Leone was an attempt to regain foreign policy credibility domestically and internationally, i.e. an act in Blair's personal political interest.

The decision to conduct Operation *Palliser* was an overall self-interested decision. Despite the existence of economic, political and geo-strategic interests, the latter were certainly the most crucial driving force behind the decision to intervene. Planned as a rescue and evacuation mission Operation *Palliser* predominantly intended to evacuate endangered British citizens. Even though the conflict in Sierra Leone has been one of the bloodiest and most severe internal conflicts of the past two decades, the British intervention in 2000 came at a time when the conflict had lost its urgency already and the country had returned to a state of relative stability. Hence, the altruistic component of this intervention was secondary to self-interested motivating factors.

3.2.9 Afghanistan (Operation Enduring Freedom, *2001)*

The terrorist attacks on September 11th 2001 triggered an immediate call within the United States for a military response. Treating these attacks conducted by Al Qaeda as comparable to a military attack, NATO regarded the incident as an actual attack against a member of the alliance and therefore called for collective self-defence.[170] A day after the attacks the UN Security Council issued Resolution 1368 (2001) condemning the attacks and expressing "[…] its readiness to take all necessary steps to respond to the terrorist attacks of 11 September 2001[…]".[171] Having identified Osama Bin Laden as the responsible decision maker behind the attacks, newly elected President Bush (jr.) confronted the Taliban regime in Afghanistan openly by demanding the extradition of Bin Laden and other Al Qaeda terrorists to US authorities. The refusal of the Taliban to do so and the call of UN SC Resolution 1373 (2001) to deny terrorist support or safe haven initiated the Bush administration to exercise its right of self-defence by intervening in Afghanistan on October 7th 2001.[172] Due to the fact that the US initially did not seek the direct assistance of NATO, I will not analyze NATO's decision making process but limit this account to the US decision making process.

Existence of an acute humanitarian crisis [1,5]

Twenty years of civil war had destroyed any semblance of functioning state structure in Afghanistan, so that in some regions clans and warlords could exercise

169 Ibid.

170 Ottaway and Lacina (2003) Op. cit. 56 (p. 81).

171 UN Security Council (2001).

172 Chesterman (2003) (p. 165).

authority without any control of the central government. The collapse of central state structure and the failure of local warlords to provide fundamental infrastructure services constantly led to a deterioration of the humanitarian situation throughout the 1990s causing more than 2.3 million Afghans to seek refuge in neighbouring countries.[173] When the Taliban erected the Islamic Emirate of Afghanistan in 1996 the humanitarian situation deteriorated further due to the oppressive nature of the Islamic fundamentalist regime enforcing the laws of the Sha'ria. Nonetheless, despite severe human rights violations such as public executions, torture or state-restricted access to medical care the situation in Afghanistan immediately prior to the US led intervention in 2001 could not be described as a supreme humanitarian emergency that was acute enough to necessitate armed intervention by the international community.[174] With the beginning of Operation *Enduring Freedom* the humanitarian situation sharply worsened, directly claiming the lives of more than 1,000 Afghanis and producing 500,000 new refugees and internally displaced persons. The destruction of infrastructure further disrupted the deliveries of food and aid causing more suffering especially in the strongly embattled areas.[175] In his address to the nation on 7 October 2001 President Bush justified intervention *inter alia* in humanitarian terms declaring that

> "[...] *the oppressed people of Afghanistan ill know the generosity of America and our allies. As we strike military targets, we'll also drop food, medicine, and supplies to the starving and suffering men and women and children of Afghanistan* [...]".[176]

Bearing in mind that President Bush never publicly addressed the humanitarian crisis in Afghanistan prior to intervention in October 2001 and knowing his stated opposition to using the US military for 'soft targets', i.e. humanitarian purposes, the credibility of this rather altruistic statement has to be questioned.[177] Only after the military leadership and the Bush administration realized the difficulty of actually capturing the most important leaders of Al Qaeda including Bin Laden, President Bush addressed the ongoing humanitarian crisis. Speaking in front of the UN in November 2001 Bush denounced the Taliban regime as terrorists promoting "[...] terror abroad and impos[ing] a reign of terror on the Afghan people [...]".[178] It is therefore most likely that the reference to the humanitarian crisis after the attack was a rather political than humanitarian move. Hence, despite the existence of a humanitarian crisis, the negligent manner with which the Bush administration addressed the crisis before and during intervention does not suggest that the crisis was the actual motivation behind intervention.

---

173 Wheeler (2004) Op. Cit. 169 (p. 13).

174 Chesterman (2003) Op. Cit. 390 (p.167).

175 McInnes (2003) (p. 180).

176 Bush (2001).

177 Wheeler (2004) Op. Cit. 169 (p. 15).

178 Bush (2001) (p. 167).

Public Awareness and Media Coverage [0]

The portrayal of the situation in Afghanistan by the US media in late 2001 was limited to the Taliban regime's involvement in supporting and harbouring Al Qaeda terrorists. Even though NGOs had repeatedly addressed the suffering of the Afghan people under the Islamic fundamentalist regime in Kabul, the media had done little to convey the message of human rights abuses to the broader US public. In fact, the "[…] picture of Afghan life painted by human rights NGOs and other informed commentators failed to capture the moral imagination of millions of Americans […]".[179] Consequently, American public opinion did not create public pressure to intervene in Afghanistan in order to improve the humanitarian situation on the ground. After the experience of 9/11 the American public was more interested to hold those accountable that were responsible for the devastating attacks in New York and Washington. As opinion polls show 88 % of all Americans were in favour of intervention but only for the purpose of averting the threat posed by the Taliban regime and Al Qaeda.[180] Hence, the American public did not trigger the Bush administration to take an altruistic decision, but on the contrary to take a decision driven by security interests.

Feeling of moral obligation to intervene by the decision-maker [0]

Taking into account that the humanitarian situation on the ground did not appear on President Bush's political agenda before September 11th, 2001, it is highly doubtful that he had personal feelings of moral obligation to intervene at any time. Evidence for any particular moral concerns for the fate of the Afghan people could not be found.

Economic Interest [0]

Evidence for economic interests at stake for the United States could not be found.

Geo-Strategic Interest [4,5]

Notwithstanding the fact that the Bush administration tried to partially rely upon a humanitarian rationale to justify the intervention in Afghanistan the prime motivator for intervention was security related. On his address to the nation on 7 October 2001 President Bush explained that the US

> "[…] *military has begun air strikes against Al Qaida terrorist training camps and military installations of the Taliban regime in Afghanistan. These carefully targeted actions are designed to disrupt the use of Afghanistan as a terrorist base of operations* […]".[181]

Thus, there is no doubt that the primary purpose of intervention was to deprive Al Qaeda of its main safe haven and training ground in order to minimize the risks of a future terrorist attack. In particular, the US military hoped to render Al Qaeda

[179] Wheeler (2004) Op. Cit. 169 (p. 37).

[180] AEI (2008) (p. 58).

[181] Bush (2001) Op. Cit. 394.

incapable of action by eliminating the leadership of the organization around Bin Laden. Drawing the connection between Al Qaeda and the Taliban regime, the Islamist government in Kabul was made indirectly responsible for the attacks of September 11th. Thereby, the US tried to legally justify intervention referring to its right of self-defence, making the entire operation geo-strategically oriented.[182] Thus, the regime of the Taliban was regarded as a threat to peace and security not because it threatened the lives of its people but because it posed a security threat to the US and its Western allies. Operation Enduring Freedom therefore served as a means of regime change opening up the way for a new regime that would allow the US direct access to terrorist hideouts.[183] Hence, it is fair to note that after the devastating experience of 9/11 the US administration had to tackle the issue of global anti-Western terrorism before acting upon any humanitarian considerations. Afghanistan thereby served as the tip of a gigantic iceberg: Depriving Al Qaeda and other terrorist groups of its operational base in Afghanistan, an objective that addressed vital geo-strategic interests at the time and served as the paramount motivation for intervention in Afghanistan.

Political Interest of the Decision Maker [2]

After the severe impact of September 11th, the US public heavily pressured the government to do something to retaliate against the attacks.[184] Newly elected President Bush had to demonstrate resolve and resoluteness in a period of national grief and feelings of insecurity. Thus, it was in Bush's personal political interest to present himself as a strong leader acting decisively against the terrorist peril believed to threaten the United States and re-establishing a sense of security in the United States. To standby passively or only using minor coercive means against Al Qaeda would have undermined Bush's credibility and would have cost him the support of the American people.

In the case of Operation *Enduring Freedom* in Afghanistan in the aftermath of September 11th, it is difficult to speak of a humanitarian intervention. Despite the claim that the intervention served *inter alia* the humanitarian purpose to bring to a halt the human rights abuses suffered by the Afghan population under the Taliban regime, the paramount motivator for US intervention was the existence of vital security interests. After the experience of 9/11 President Bush had to do something to show the American public that he was determined to bring the perpetrators to justice. It seems as if the humanitarian rationale was utilized by the Bush administration to present a just cause for an otherwise self-interested intervention.

---

182 Chesterman (2003) Op. Cit. 390 (p. 174).

183 McInnes (2003) Op. Cit. 393 (p. 175).

184 AEI (2008) Op. Cit. 398 (p. 58).

3.2.10 *Iraq (Operation* **Iraqi Freedom***, 2003)*

Probably the most controversial use of force in the post Cold War era was the US led intervention in Iraq 2003. In the aftermath of 9/11 and the commencing war on terror in Afghanistan two years earlier the United States were still highly concerned about Saddam Hussein's regime. Iraq's program to develop weapons of mass destruction (WMD) had been under supervision of the UN and IAEA until 1998 when Iraq expelled the UN weapon inspectors. Iraq's continuous failure to cooperate with UN authorities and IAEA inspectors and to allow them unrestricted access to possible production sides of WMDs triggered the UN Security Council to issue Resolution 1441 (2002) granting Iraq thirty days to reveal all aspects of the weapon development program. Further UN SC Resolution 1441 (2002) decided

> "[...] *that Iraq has been and remains in material breach of its obligations under relevant resolutions, including resolution 687 (1991), in particular through Iraq's failure to cooperate with United Nations inspectors and the IAEA* [...]"[185]

before stating

> "[...] *that false statements or omissions in the declarations submitted by Iraq* [...] *and failure by Iraq at any time to comply with, and cooperate fully in the implementation of, this resolution shall constitute a further material breach of Iraq's obligations* [...]".[186]

Without stating explicitly how the international community would react to Iraq's non-compliance, this resolution nonetheless created a clear obligation for Iraq to comply. The failure to comply with UN SC Resolution 1441 (2002) and the establishment of the fact that Iraq was in material breach of several obligations was enough for the US to put together a force to intervene in Iraq on March 20th, 2003, even though the UN Security Council did not authorize such an action. In this book I will analyze the motivations for the US to intervene as the leading military power in Operation *Iraqi Freedom.*

Existence of an acute humanitarian crisis [1]

Even though the Bush administration retroactively tried to create a humanitarian justification for intervention, the crisis in Iraq in 2003 was far from being a supreme humanitarian emergency in comparison to the regime's massive human rights abuses against ethnic minorities or political opponents in the 1980s or beginning 1990s. Throughout the 25 year reign of the Ba'th Party approximately 250,000 Iraqis were killed by the regime whereby the *Anfal* massacre against Kurds in 1988 killing more than 100,000 people was the most severe humanitarian crisis. "Brutal as Saddam Hussein's reign had been, the scope of the Iraqi government's killing in March 2003 was not of the exceptional and dire magnitude

---

[185] UN Security Council (2002).

[186] Ibid.

that would justify humanitarian intervention [...]".[187] Thus, the humanitarian situation in 2003 characterized by arbitrary arrests and killings was not acute and the extent of the crisis did not constitute a supreme humanitarian emergency.[188] As the crisis between the US and Iraq about WMDs further unfolded and US intervention become more likely, the Bush administration also began using a humanitarian rationale to support the cause for intervention hoping that the relatively sceptical international community might become more supportive of a military solution. In particular when the reference to WMDs became more elusive and criticism about the validity of the *casus belli* arose, those in favour of removing Saddam Hussein relied increasingly on humanitarian rationales.[189] *Inter alia* President Bush declared in his address to the nation on March 17th, 2003 that

> "[...] *As our coalition takes away their power, we will deliver the food and medicine you need. We will tear down the apparatus of terror, and we will help you to build a new Iraq that is prosperous and free. In a free Iraq, there will be no more wars of aggression against your neighbors, no more poison factories, no more executions of dissidents, no more torture chambers and rape rooms. The tyrant will soon be gone. The day of your liberation is near* [...]".[190]

The removal of Hussein's regime was continuously interpreted by the Bush administration as the 'liberation' of the Iraqi people from suppression and state terror. Additionally, the US promised to supply Iraq with necessary food and medicine supplies. Despite the attempt by the Bush administration to defend intervention on humanitarian grounds, the absence of an acute humanitarian crisis and the relatively weak public reference to the crisis prior to 2002 makes the humanitarian motivation and intention of the US highly incredible.

Public Awareness and Media Coverage [0]

Global media coverage of the crisis in Iraq in the years prior to the intervention was dominated by 'the cat-and-mouse game' between the Iraqi government and UN weapons inspectors. The long record of gross human rights abuses that had dominated the media coverage on Iraq during the 1990s did not receive a considerable amount of attention. In the aftermath of September 11th and the war on terror Iraq suddenly became an interesting topic for both political leaders and the media. When the Bush administration started to gather and present evidence for the existence of WMDs in Iraq that could potentially threaten the US homeland, the US media jumped on the bandwagon. Doubtful facts presented as evidence by members of the Bush administration such as Collin Powell who gave an infamous speech at the UN Security Council on February 3rd, 2003 were channelled uncritically to the consumer.[191] Thereby, the justifications for intervening in Iraq

---

[187] Roth (2004) (p. 6).

[188] Bellamy (2004) Op. Cit. 219 (p. 137).

[189] Wheeler and Bellamy (2008) Op. Cit. 44 (p. 573).

[190] Bush (2003).

[191] Ravi (2005).(p. 49).

induced by the Bush administration were to a large extent adopted by the editorials of the biggest newspapers in the US. Not exposed to any humanitarian calls for intervention 88 % of the US public were convinced in 2003 that something had to be done about Hussein's regime in Iraq as it was believed to support terrorists groups and to plan attacks against the US. Further, the same poll conducted by CNN/USA Today/Gallup revealed that 51 % of all Americans believed that Saddam Hussein was directly involved in the 9/11 terror attacks.[192] Hence, pubic support for intervention in Iraq 2003 was triggered by declared security concerns and did not show any altruistic component.

Feeling of moral obligation to intervene by the decision-maker [0]

Evidence for personal compassionate feelings by President Bush for the Iraqi people's fate could not be found.

Economic Interest [4]

As one of the oil richest countries in the world Iraq has always been of significant economic importance for the West.[193] Removing Saddam Hussein's regime from power meant that the US had access to the former nationalized oil fields in Iraq. Among the many US American companies engaged in the reconstruction of Iraq after the intervention the oilfield services cooperation Halliburton takes up a special role. Formerly chaired by Vice President Richard Chaney, Halliburton was awarded with government contracts worth $ 8 billion making the company and its value grow. Chaney who had been compensated with a considerable amount of shares after leaving the company in 2000 directly profited from Halliburton's preferential treatment.[194] Apart from this particular example the Bush administration had a special interest in boosting its economy by allowing US mineral resource extraction companies and private military and security companies to benefit from post-war reconstruction.[195]

Geo-Strategic Interest [5]

After 9/11 President Bush immediately referred to Hussein's regime in Baghdad as a rogue regime and placed it together with North Korea and Iran on the 'Axis of Evil'.[196] The intervention in Iraq was predominantly driven by conventional security-related geo-strategic interests. In his address to the nation on March 17th, 2003 President Bush declared that "[…] The United States of America has […] to use force in assuring its own national security […]".[197] The belief that Iraq had the potential to construct WMDs and was not afraid to employ them against the US or

---

[192] Norris et al. (2003).(p. 39).

[193] CIA (2010).

[194] Bjorna (2009) Op. Cit. 38 (p. 128).

[195] Mednicoff (2006) Op. Cit. 89 (p. 391).

[196] Bellamy (2004) Op. Cit. 219 (p. 135).

[197] Bush (2003) Op. Cit. 408.

other vital Western targets, created a perceived security threat that could not have been disregarded after the experience of 9/11. Further, Iraq was of major interest in the war against terror as it allegedly supported and hosted Al Qaeda and other Islamic terrorist organizations, a claim that was only raised after the intervention started. A reality where terrorists could have access to WMDs was unacceptable for the US.[198] Thus, Operation *Iraqi Freedom* was designed as a pre-emptive strike of self-defence so as to foreclose a potential attack from Saddam Hussein. Along with the goal of eliminating the security threat the Bush administration was particularly interested in finally bringing about a regime change in Iraq after decades of violence and misgovernment.[199] Establishing a just and liberal multi-party democracy in Iraq was believed to enhance the creation of a democratic Iraqi society facilitating foreign and trade relations for Western states in the region.[200] As it is difficult to assess the trustworthiness and the validity of the claims raised by the US government, it remains impossible to explicitly state which of the justifications were fabricated allegations and which were the actual factors that motivated the US government to intervene. Nonetheless, the literature seems to suggest that the War in Iraq was mainly driven by conventional security maximizing interests.

Political Interest of the Decision Maker [2,5]

With midterm elections coming up towards the end of 2002 the Bush administration had to present a determined, coherent and credible approach to the situation in Iraq. Having made severe allegations against the regime in Baghdad, the President had to act in order to convince the electorate that he as the President was capable of dealing with this security threat. Moreover, President Bush was looking for a place in the history books that could only be granted by a successful foreign policy decision. A strike against his created 'Axis of Evil' was important and Iraq seemed to offer the best conditions for a quick and achievable operation. Accordingly, President Bush's decision to intervene in Iraq was partially also driven by his own political interest.[201]

Operation *Iraqi Freedom* cannot be defined as a humanitarian intervention. The reason is that it lacks any altruistic component. Apart from strong US economic interests in Iraq, the Bush administration was mainly driven security maximizing interests in the realist sense of the word. As a part of the 'Axis of Evil' Saddam Hussein's regime posed a potential security threat to the region as well as indirectly to the United States. Primarily, Saddam Hussein's government constituted a rogue regime that had repeatedly defied the will of the international community and had become a potential threat for the United States at a time that America was trapped in security paranoia. If the intervention was predominantly motivated by economic interests, the United States would have intervened long before March 2003.

---

198 Acharya (2003) Op. Cit. 146 (p. 1).

199 Gleddisch et al. (1997) Op. Cit. 278 (p. 15).

200 Bjorna (2009) Op. Cit. 38 (p. 130).

201 Ibid (p. 132).

3.2.11 Rwanda (Non-Intervention, 1994)

Three years of civil war between the two major ethnic groups in Rwanda, the Hutu and the Tutsi, had been brought to an end by the international community with the signature of the Arusha Accords 1993. Instead of soothing tensions deeply rooted in a history of ethnic collusion between the Hutu and Tutsi, the Arusha Accords added fuel to the flames as they were badly mediated and did not satisfy the demands of both parties.[202] In the months following the signature of the Accords the UN Peacekeeping Force UNAMIR,[203] which deployed to supervise the implementation of the Accords, witnessed increasing tensions between the ethnic groups. Despite warnings by UNAMIR's General Dallaire that militias supported by the Hutu government were preparing genocide against the Tutsis minority, the international community did little to act on these notes. When the Hutu President Habyarimana's plane was shot down over Kigali Airport on April 6th 1994, the retained aggression and hatred against the perceived 'aliens', the Tutsis, erupted into genocide aiming at the extinction of the entire Tutsi population.[204] Rather than living up to their mandate and protect civilians UNAMIR's strength was reduced to 270 troops and General Dallaire had to stand by passively watching hundreds of thousands of Tutsis getting slaughtered.[205] French intervention under Operation *Turquoise* came three months too late and the question remains why the international community did not act earlier. Having analyzed the French motivation to act in July 1994, this section will try to analyze the motivations behind the American decision to abstain from intervention in April 1994—a decision that arguably cost the lives of approximately 300,000 people.[206]

Existence of an acute humanitarian crisis [4]

The genocide in Rwanda certainly satisfied the criteria for a supreme humanitarian emergency as "[…] the survival of populations and entire ethnic groups [was] seriously compromised […]".[207] Within three months more than 800,000 people were slaughtered using primitive weapons such as machetes, making it the worst genocide in terms of casualties per time in the history of mankind.[208] In fact it is commonly acknowledged that "[…] the most remarkable aspect of the genocide was its speed […]".[209] In addition to the vitiation of more than 11 % of the entire population within weeks more than 2 million individuals were displaced seeking

---

202 Lemarchand (2006) Op. Cit. 283 (p. 6).

203 UNAMIR = United Nations Assistance Mission for Rwanda.

204 Grünfeld (2007) Op. Cit. 64 (p. 92).

205 Barnett (2002) Op. Cit. 286 (p. 76).

206 Kuperman (2000) Op. Cit. 289 (p. 110).

207 Bellamy (2004) Op. Cit. 219 (p. 138).

208 Kuperman (2000) Op. Cit. 289 (p. 98).

209 Ibid (p.96).

refuge in the neighbouring states of the Great Lakes region.[210] There is no doubt that the humanitarian situation in April 1994 was catastrophic and acuter than in the months to come since most of the killings were committed already within the first four weeks. Despite this supreme humanitarian emergency, President Clinton did little to address the crisis appropriately using the right terminology. By the end of April the Clinton administration had been informed about the extent of the atrocities and was fully aware of the fact that hundreds of thousands had been killed by the Hutu militias constituting genocide and not civil war.[211] Nonetheless, in a public statement on April 30th, 1994 President Clinton referred to the atrocities committed as "[...] the horrors of civil war [...]"[212] and calls upon both the Hutu militia and the Tutsi Rwandan People's Front, which intervened from the North to stop the unilateral violence, to agree on an immediate cease-fire. Thereby Clinton gave the US public the illusion that the crisis in Rwanda was just another civil war. Throughout the genocide in 1994 President Clinton intentionally avoided the term genocide knowing that it would obligate the international community to intervene. In so doing Clinton failed to make a credible and suitable reference to the crisis.[213]

Public Awareness and Media Coverage [0]

The media played a particular role in the response to the humanitarian crisis in Rwanda. The media both in Europe and the US failed to do justice to its role as an agenda setter as it failed to create public awareness for the urgency of the human suffering on the ground. While the US media remained relatively silent when the atrocities began in the beginning of April, towards the end of the month the media had managed to redirect the focus away from the ongoing genocide to the arising refugee crisis caused by the mass killings. As a result, the Rwandan crisis was remembered by the public as people who die of cholera.[214] Covering the misery of the refugees in the camps in Goma, the media increased public awareness, however, did not increase the public's knowledge of what caused the mass exodus.[215] Not knowing the cause for the refugee crisis in Zaire and fed by unqualified statements by the media and NGOs the US public did not develop a sensitivity for the crisis. In fact, US public opinion was relatively disinterested in the beginning believing that the delivery of humanitarian aid would ameliorate the situation on the ground. When it became obvious in the beginning of June 1994 that the humanitarian crisis in Zaire was a result of mass killings in Rwanda, 63 % of the US public stated clearly in opinion polls that Rwanda did not touch upon vital US interests and that it would be therefore wrong to risk the lives of American

---

210 Magnarella (2005) Op. Cit 291 (p. 816).

211 Barnett (1997).(p. 575).

212 Clinton (1994).

213 Barnett (1997) Op.Cit. 429 (p. 575).

214 Mackintosh (1996).(p. 337).

215 Hilsum (1996).

troops.[216] Hence, not only did the US public not pressure the government to intervene to save lives but it actually opposed intervention based on the then recent memory of losing American soldiers in a war of choice in Somalia. Therefore, the US leadership was convinced that intervention was against the public will in America.[217]

Feeling of moral obligation to intervene by the decision-maker [0]

Evidence for personal compassionate feelings by President Clinton for the fate of the Rwandan Tutsis could not be found. Personal compassionate feelings would have caused President Clinton to address the crisis more harshly and push both the public and Congress to allow for humanitarian intervention.

Economic Interest [0]

> "[…] *Few countries are less* [economically] *significant than Rwanda. No precious or strategic minerals have been discovered there, nor is it located on any "arc of crisis" or near any choke point for navigation.* […it is] *no larger than Maryland and landlocked with the nearest port more than six hundred miles away* […]".[218]

This statement shows that the US could not have had any economic or trade interests at stake in Rwanda, an economy that was predominately based on subsistence agriculture.

Geo-Strategic Interest [0,5]

With the end of the Cold War US geo-strategic interests in sub-Saharan Africa dropped drastically in the early 1990s. Prior to the war against global terrorism the Great Lakes region in particular did not pose any threat to US security interests making Rwanda strategically insignificant.[219] The only remaining national interest in Rwanda in April 1994 was to rescue US citizens from Kigali. President Clinton stated that "[…] all Americans out immediately […]"[220] was the ultimate priority. With the French army coordinating the evacuation from Kigali Airport in the first week of the genocide, the United State's state obligation to protect its citizens abroad was fulfilled.

Political Interest of the Decision Maker [0]

Facing public and political opposition to intervening in Rwanda it was in Clinton's political interest not to intervene. In particular Republicans in Congress strongly pressured Clinton to get less involved in humanitarian operations.[221] After the experience of Somalia and the premature withdrawal of US troops Clinton was in

---

216 Shibata (2006) Op. Cit. 156 (p. 19).

217 Ibid (p.18).

218 Wrage (2000).

219 McQueen (2006) Op. Cit. 47 (p. 105).

220 Grünfeld (2007) Op. Cit. 64 (p. 170).

221 Ibid (p. 142).

urgent need for a positive foreign policy initiative. Intervening in Rwanda did not promise to be a quick and easy peacekeeping operation but a rather long term commitment involving high costs of money and lives.[222] Thus, intervention would have gone against Clinton's political interest.

The humanitarian crisis in Rwanda 1994 is a clear case of a Western state, e.g. the United States, confronted with a humanitarian catastrophe in absence of vital national interests. From all intervention and non-intervention cases examined in this book, the case of Rwanda presents the lowest degree of self-interest. In absence of media coverage and public awareness, the crisis in Rwanda was not on the agenda of most Western governments until streams of refugees were arriving in the border regions of Zaire and Uganda. Even after the full extent of the atrocities committed by the Hutus became obvious, the lack of national/self-interest for the US government obstructed intervention. Altruism alone does not trigger intervention.

3.2.12 Darfur (Non-Intervention, 2003 ff.)

Against the backdrop of years of fighting between the Arab North (the government) and the rebelling African South, violence erupted in the region of Darfur. Darfur constitutes a large area in Western Sudan whose population can be characterized as a complex tribal mix. Even though a great majority of over 70 % of the population adheres to Islam and speaks Arabic, ethnically the population is divided into Black Africans and Arabs.[223] Coexisting peacefully for centuries it was a pro-Arabic policy shift in the capital Khartoum that brought about a process of 'unmixing' resulting in social tensions within Sudan's Western province.[224] In addition to famines and constant supply shortages "[…] a dismissive Arab supremacist ideology […]"[225] spread by the Sudanese government caused ethnic upheavals. Founded to tackle government oppression, the Black-African Sudanese Liberation Army (SLA) launched several attacks against government and army institutions in Darfur in 2002. The government in Khartoum retaliated using both army troops and local Arab militias, called the *janjawid*, hitting SLA hide outs with destructive force.[226] The UN Security Council reacted to the occurring ethnic violence in 2004 by adopting UN SC Resolution 1556 (2004) harshly condemning all acts of violence and "[…] determining that the situation in Sudan constitutes a threat to international peace and security and to stability in the region […]".[227]

[222] Ibid (p. 143).

[223] Hagan and Rymond-Richmond (2009) (p. 109).

[224] Prunier (2007) (p. 5).

[225] Hagan and Rymond-Richmond Op. Cit. 441 (p. 112).

[226] Daly (2007) (p.282).

[227] UN Security Council (2004).

Despite the knowledge about and condemnation of the atrocities committed in Darfur the UN Security Council did not do more than authorizing the deployment of international monitors to the Darfur region. In the following years the UN was not able to agree on the authorization of an intervention force to stop the continuing violence even though the international community was highly committed to establish long-lasting peace in Southern Sudan. UN SC Resolution 1593 (2005) addressed the gross human rights abuses by filing charges against the identified perpetrators in front of the ICC. In 2007 the UN authorized the African Union with the creation of a 27,000 troops-strong peace keeping force for Darfur.[228] Notwithstanding the fact that the extent of the atrocities and the urgency of the humanitarian situation were well known, the international community did not decide to intervene to bring the suffering to an end. As the main power strongly addressing and condemning the humanitarian catastrophe the US's motivation not to intervene in Darfur will be analyzed in this section.

Existence of an acute humanitarian crisis [5]

Since the eruption of violence between SLA militias and government forces in March 2003 the humanitarian situation on the ground in Darfur had constantly deteriorated over the years. Confronted with a militia group such as the SLA employing guerrilla tactics the Sudanese government was seeking for an efficient military solution to the problem. The *janjawid*, Arab militias operating in Darfur, were supported by the government with arms, ammunition and air strikes in order to fight against Black African civilians who were believed to host SLA militias.[229] In its World Report 2005 Human Rights Watch described the humanitarian situation in Darfur as follows:

> "[…]*The Janjaweed and Sudanese armed forces continued a campaign begun in earnest in* 2003 *of ethnic cleansing and forced displacement by bombing and burning villages, killing civilians, and raping women. The first half of* 2004 *saw a dramatic increase in these atrocities. By year's end hundreds of villages were destroyed, an estimated* 2 *million civilians were forcibly displaced by the government of Sudan and its militias, and* 70,000 *died as a direct or indirect cause of this campaign* […]".[230]

The death toll has constantly risen over the years reaching approximately 300,000 at the end of 2005 while millions were driven from their land by mass killings, rapes and mutilations making the crisis in Darfur the "[…] worst humanitarian disaster on the planet […]"[231] at the time. Thus, the humanitarian situation in Darfur since 2003 doubtlessly constituted a supreme humanitarian emergency. Unlike in previous humanitarian crises the US administration has addressed and condemned the violence harshly from the beginning. After visiting the Darfur region in 2004 Secretary of State Powell delivered a speech in

[228] UNAMID (2009).

[229] Straus (2005).(p. 127).

[230] HRW (2005) (p. 166).

[231] Straus (2005) Op. Cit. 447 (p. 123).

September 2004 where he publicly called upon the government of Sudan to disarm the militia and allow foreign aid to come in. Powell continues by stating "[...] that genocide has been committed in Darfur and that the Government of Sudan and the jinjaweid bear responsibility [...]".[232] For the first time in history a member of a US government used the term 'genocide' to refer to an act committed by another government. In spite of Powell's explicit statement he managed to bend the Genocide Convention in a way that the US would not have to act on her genocide allegations raised against Sudan. Nonetheless, Powell called on the United Nations to bring further pressure to bear.[233] Hence, both the existence of an acute humanitarian crisis as well as the acknowledgment of the crisis by the US government suggests that a reasonable degree of altruism was involved in dealing with the crisis.

Public Awareness and Media Coverage [2,5]

In comparison to other humanitarian crises presented earlier in this book the extent of the atrocities committed and the human suffering on the ground in Darfur was very well documented and publicised. Apart from NGOs such Human Rights Watch, Amnesty International or International Crisis Group also big newspapers such as the *New York Times* had covered the conflict in Darfur in detail.[234] Both the media coverage and reports released by major human rights NGOs created a public awareness of the crisis in Darfur as early as 2004. The American public showed support for a variety of possible steps in the response to the crisis including the option to use forceful intervention to bring the humanitarian crisis to an end. An opinion poll conducted in 2005 revealed that in face of the severity of the humanitarian crisis 61 % of the US public approved the use of military force to stop the violence in Darfur.[235] Hence, the attention of the media and especially the campaigning of major NGOs created a public awareness in the US calling on the government to do something to relieve the suffering of Darfurians.

Feeling of moral obligation to intervene by the decision-maker [0]

Even though there is no evidence that any other member of the Bush administration was emotionally touched by the humanitarian crisis or even felt morally obliged to act on the crisis, US Secretary of State Powell as well as his successor Rice travelled to the region and witnessed the misery both in Darfur and in the refugee camps in Chad. Witnessing the atrocities and the human suffering in midsummer, Powell returned to the US to deliver his speech condemning the mass killings and calling upon the international community to put pressure on the government in Khartoum.[236] However, there is no record explicitly stating that

[232] US Department of State (2004).

[233] Williams and Bellamy (2005).(p. 31).

[234] Grono (2006).(p. 625).

[235] PIPA (2005).(p. 4).

[236] HRW (2005) Op. Cit. 448 (p. 34).

Powell was driven in his decisions by compassionate feelings that were triggered by witnessing the atrocities first hand.

Economic Interest [1,5]

Sudan, covering an area almost as big as Western Europe, is rich of a variety of natural resources, among them oil and natural gas, two resources of crucial US economic interest.[237] However, due to economic sanctions set up by the Clinton administration in 1997 US petroleum companies highly interested in new exploitation grounds could not take advantage of Sudan's and Darfur's lucrative geological conditions. Thus, with sanctions still prohibiting trade with Sudan, the US did not have any investments at stake in any part of Sudan.[238] Instead China had invested billions of dollars into the oil industry in Sudan making it Sudan's most important export partner.[239] Intervening forcefully in Darfur to bring the atrocities to a halt and to stabilize the region might have been economically beneficial for US companies that were and still are eager to explore new drilling grounds. Nonetheless, economic interests in Sudan were rather peripheral at the time since the US economy was not reliant upon Sudanese exports.

Geo-Strategic Interest [0]

Sudan, a country famous for granting safe haven to terrorists for a long time, became of particular strategic interest to the US after 9/11 and within the framework of the War on Terror. Having implemented Arabization policies and having adopted Islamic fundamentalist *Shari'a*-based legislation the government in Khartoum had chosen a political agenda that was alarming for US counter-terrorist institutions.[240] Within the framework of the War on Terror the US had managed to persuade the Sudanese government to be more cooperative with US anti-terror policies, bringing about the expulsion of Al Qaeda figure heads and the closure of terrorist training camps.[241] The cooperation between US American and Sudanese intelligence went even that far that senior Sudanese government officials, among them architects of the mass killings in Darfur, were flown out to Virginia in 2005 to meet with officials of the CIA.[242] Hence, having established important strategic ties with the government in Khartoum it was actually in the geo-strategic interest of the US not to intervene in Darfur so as not to jeopardize the progress made in the fight against terror.

---

[237] CIA (2010)

[238] Martin (2002) (p. 126).

[239] Grono (2006) Op. Cit. 452 (p. 628).

[240] Daly (2007) Op. Cit. 444 (p. 261).

[241] Blunt (2004).

[242] Grono (2006) Op. Cit. 452 (p. 628).

Table 3.1 below presents an overview over all of the parameter values derived from the 15 cases

	Public awareness and media coverage	Existence of an acute humanitarian crisis	Feeling of moral obligation to intervene by the decision-maker	Total amount altruism	Economic interest	Geo-strategic interest	Political interest of the decision maker	Total amount national interest
Northern Iraq	3.5	2.5	1	7	0	4	1	5
Somalia	2.5	4.5	4	11	1.5	0	4	5.5
Haiti	2	3	0	5	3	3	3	9
Rwanda (FR)	0.5	3	0	3.5	0	5	2.5	7.5
Bosnia	3	4	0	7	1.5	4	2.5	8
Kosovo	1.5	3	0	4.5	0	4.5	1	5.5
East Timor	4.5	4	0	8.5	2.5	3.5	1	7
Sierra Leone	1	2.5	2	5.5	1.5	4	2	7.5
Afghanistan	0	1.5	0	1.5	0	4.5	2	6.5
Iraq	0	1	0	1	4	5	2.5	11.5
Rwanda (US)	0	4	0	4	0	0,5	0	0.5
Darfur	2.5	5	0	7.5	1.5	0	0.5	2

Political Interest of the Decision Maker [0,5]

With the American public supporting humanitarian intervention it would have been in the political interest of the Bush administration to intervene in Darfur in order to satisfy the electorate. However, as the public pressure was apparently not considered to be compelling enough to overrule strong geo-strategic interests not to intervene, the degree of political interest at stake has to be considered minimal.

The humanitarian crisis in Darfur represents another case of an endangered population being exposed to the arbitrariness of genocidaries in a region where US national/self-interests were absent. Clearly, the high degree of altruism on its own was not sufficient for the US administration to consider intervention despite the fact that the extent of the suffering was publicly known. Minimal economic interests, the absence of geo-strategic interests in a sub-Saharan country and close ties between the United States and the government in Khartoum in the War against Terror made any coercive intervention into the crisis impossible.

3.2.13 Overview of Intervention and Non-Intervention Cases

Overview of intervention and non-intervention cases as shown in Table 3.1.

References

Bellamy AJ (2004) Ethics and intervention: the ‘humanitarian exception’ and the problem of abuse in the case of Iraq. J Peace Res 41:131. Sage Publications, London

Walzer M (1977) Just and unjust wars, 1st edn. Basic Books, New York

Ottaway M, Lacina B (2003) International interventions and imperialism: lessons from the 1990s. SAIS Rev XXIII(2) (Summer–Fall 2003). John Hopkins University Press, Washington

Walzer M (1995) The politics of rescue. Soc Res 62(1):51ff. The New School of Social Research, New York

Jakobsen PV (1996) National interest, humanitarianism or CNN: what triggers UN peace enforcement after the cold war? J Peace Res 33(2):205–215. Sage Publications, London (May 1996)

Roberts A (1993) Humanitarian war: military intervention and human rights. Int Aff (Roy Inst Int Aff 1944) 69(3):429–449. Blackwell Publishing, London (Jul 1993)

Ryter MA (2003) Motives for humanitarian intervention and the international community. National Defence College/ Maanpuolustuskorkeakoulu, Helsinki

FT (1991) Bush rejects call for US intervention in Iraq. Pearson, London. Financial Times, 2 April 1991

Wheeler N (2002). Saving strangers: humanitarian intervention in international society. Oxford University Press, Oxford

Mandelbaum M (1994) The reluctance to intervene. Foreign Policy 95(Summer):3–18. The Slate Group, Washington

Kirişçi K (1996) Security for states vs. refugees: operation provide comfort and the April 1991 mass influx of refugees from northern Iraq into Turkey. Refuge 15(3). Centre for Refugee Studies, York University, Toronto. Jun 1996

Stuckey ME (1992) Remembering the future: rhetorical echoes of world war II and Vietnam in George Bush's public speech on the Gulf War. Commun Stud 43(4):246–256. Routledge Publisher, London. Winter 1992

MacFarlane SN, Weiss T (2000) Political interest and humanitarian action. Secur Stud 10(1):112–142. Routledge, London

Livingston S (1997) Clarifying the CNN effect: an examination of media effects according to type of military intervention. Joan Shorenstein Barone center on the press, politics and public policy, research paper R-18

Durch W (1996) Introduction to anarchy: humanitarian intervention and "state building" in Somalia. In: Durch William (ed) UN peacekeeping, American policy and the Uncivil Wars of the 1990s. St Martin's Press, New York

Pilger J (1993) The US fraud in Africa. New statesman and society. New Statesman, London. 8 Jan 1993

UN Security Council (1992). 3145th meeting. Resolution 794 (1992). Available: Readex/Index to United Nations Documents and Publication. (S/RES/794). 3 December 1992

Lofland VJ (2003) Somalia: U.S. intervention and operation restore hope. Air war college publication. Maxwell, AL: Air War College. Retrieved 18th October 2009 from www.au.af.mil/au/awc/awcgate/navy/pmi/somalia1.pdf

Glanville L (2005). Somalia reconsidered: an examination of the norm of humanitarian intervention. J Humanitarian Assistance, The Feinstein International Center, Medford, MA September 2005

Bush GHW (1992) Address on somalia. Miller center of public affairs. Retrieved 19th October 2009 from http://millercenter.org/scripps/archive/speeches/detail/3984

Robinson P (2001) Operation restore hope and the illusion of a news media driven intervention. Political Stud 49:941–956. Blackwell Studies, London

Natsios A (1996) Illusions of influence: the CNN effect in complex emergencies. In: Robert I, Rotberg and Thomas G Weiss (eds.) From massacres to genocide, The media, public policy and humanitarian crises. The Brookings Institute, Washington

DiPrizio RC (2002) Armed humanitarians: US interventions from northern Iraq to Kosovo. John Hopkins University Press, London

Woods JL (1997) U.S. government decision-making processes during humanitarian operations in somalia. In: Clarke Walter, Herbst Jeffrey (eds) Learning from somalia: the lessons of armed humanitarian intervention. Westview Press, London

Havel V (1999) Kosovo and the end of the nation-state. Translated by Paul Wilson. New York Review of Books 46(10):4–6. New York: NYREV, (June 10)

Fineman M (1993) The oil factor in somalia. The Los Angeles Times, The Times Mirror Company, Los Angeles, CA 18, Jan 1993

Finnemore M (2003) The purpose of intervention. Cornell University Press, NY

Wheeler N (2003) The humanitarian responsibilities of sovereignty: explaining the development of a new norm of military intervention for humanitarian purposes in international society. In: Welsh JM (ed) Humanitarian intervention and international relations. Oxford University Press, Oxford

Edwards JA (2008) Defining the enemy for the post-cold war world: Bill Clinton's foreign policy discourse in Somalia and Haiti. Int J Commun 2:830–847. University of Southern California, Los Angeles, CA

UN Security Council (1994) 3413th meeting. Resolution 940 (1994). Available: Readex/Index to United Nations Documents and Publication. (S/RES/940). 31 July 1994

CJA (2009) Haiti 1991–1994: death squads and state violence under the military regime. The centre for justice and accountability. Retrieved January 1st, 2010 from http://www.cja.org/article.php?list=type&type=250

Grünholz A (2005) State- und nation-building in der amerikanischen Außenpolitik am Beispiel Haiti [state and nation building as pat of the US foreign policy illustrated on basis of the example 'Haiti]. MA thesis in latin american studies. Universität zu Köln, Forschungsinstitut für politische Wissenschaft und Europäische Fragen. Cologne University, Cologne, GER

Clinton WJ (1994) Address to the nation on Haiti. The public papers of the president 1558–1562. The United States Government Printing Office, Washington (15 Sep 1994)

Goddard BP (1997) Military peacekeeping operations in Haiti. Global security report 1997. Alexandria, VA: global security.Org. Retrieved October 15th 2009 from http://www.globalsecurity.org/military/library/report/1997/Goddard.htm

Rudolf P (2000) Friedenserhaltung und Friedenserzwingung: Militärinterventionen in der amerikanischen Außenpolitik. In: Peter Rudolf, Jürgen Wilzewski (eds.) Weltmacht ohne Gegner. Amerikanische Außenpolitik zu Beginn des 21. Jahrhunderts. Baden Baden, GER: Nomos

Martin C (1997) President Clinton's Haiti Dilemma, pew case studies in international affairs, institute for the study of diplomacy, school of foreign service. Georgetown University, Washington

Mandelbaum M (1996) Foreign policy as social work. Foreign Aff 75(1):6–32. Council on Foreign Relations, Washington (Jan–Feb. 1996)

Blakely M (1999) Haiti. In: Brown EM, Rosecrance RM (eds) The costs of conflict: prevention and cure in the global arena. Rowman and Littlefield, Plymouth

Gleddisch NP et al (1997) Democratic Jihad? military intervention and democracy. World bank policy research working paper 4242. World Bank Publications, Washington June 2007

Robyn P (2001) The united states and Haiti (1993–1994). Wodrow Wilson school case study no. 1/2001. Princeton University, Princeton, NJ

Lemarchand R (2006) Consociationalism and power sharing in Africa: Rwanda, Burundi, and the democratic republic of the Congo. Oxford University Press, Oxford

Grünfeld F (2007) The failure to prevent genocide in Rwanda; the role of bystanders. Brill, Leiden

Barnett M (2002) Eyewitness to a genocide; the united nations and Rwanda. Cornell University Press, London

UN Security Council (1994) 3392th meeting. Resolution 929 (1994). Available: Readex/Index to United Nations Documents and Publication. (S/RES/929). 22 June 1994

Kuperman A (2000) Rwanda in retrospect. Foreign Aff 79(1) (Jan–Feb 2000). Council on Foreign Relations, New York, pp. 94–118

Magnarella PJ(2005) The background and the causes of the genocide in Rwanda. J Int Criminal Justice 3:801–822. Oxford University Press, Oxford

Wheeler N, Bellamy A (2008) Humanitarian intervention in world politics. In: John Baylis, Steve Smith (eds) The globalization of world politics: an introduction to international relations, Oxford University Press, Oxford p 525

CEC (2004) Rapport de la CEC sur la motivation de l'opération Turquoise. La Commission d'Enquête Citoyenne pour la vérité sur l'implication française dans le génocide des Tutsi. Paris: CEC. Retrieved 25 October 2009 on http://cec.rwanda.free.fr/documents/Publications/Version-Html/k_lc26marsTur.htm

Jaboeuf V (2008) French complicity in the Rwandan genocide: an interview with Jean-Paul Gouteux. World politics review, 15 April 2008. Washington, DC: WPR. Retrieved online, 10 January 2010 from http://www.worldpoliticsreview.com/Article.aspx?id=1940

McQueen C (2006) Humanitarian intervention and safety zones: Iraq, Bosnia and Rwanda. Palgrave, London

CIA (2010) Rwanda, the economy—overview. The world fact book. Updated January 5, 2010. Langley, VA: The central intelligence agency. Retrieved 10 January 2010 from https://www.cia.gov/library/publications/the-world-factbook/geos/rw.html

Klinghoffer AJ (1998) The international dimension of genocide in Rwanda. New York University Press, New York

Owen RC (2001) Operation deliberate force: a case study on humanitarian constraints in aerospace warfare. Working paper workshop: humanitarian challenges in military intervention. Havard Kennedy School, CARR Center for Human Rights Policy, Cambridge, MA

Jehl D (1994) Conflict in the balkans; Clinton outlines U.S. Interest in bosnia air strikes. The New York Times, New York: The New York Times Company, 10 Feb 1994

Clinton WJ (1995) Remarks on the agreement to end air strikes in bosnia and an exchange with reporters, 15 Sep 1995. The American presidency project. Retrieved online October 24, 2009 from http://www.presidency.ucsb.edu/ws/index.php?pid=51846&st=&st1

Höges C (1995) Peitsche und Zuckerbrot. Der SPIEGEL 36:22–25. Hamburg: Spiegel Verlag

Lucarelli S (2000) Europe and the breakup of Yugoslavia: a political failure in search of a scholarly explanation. Kluwer Law International, The Hague, NL p 34

Cohn M (2003) The myth of humanitarian intervention in Kosovo. In: Aleksandar Jokic (ed.) Lessons of Kosovo: the dangers of humanitarian intervention, Broadview Press, Peterborough, ON p 122

Murray-Miller G (2007) Beyond tragedy: NATO's intervention in the former Yugoslavia. Hindsight graduate history J Spring 1 California State University, Fresno, CA

Clinton WJ (2004) My life. Alfred A Knopf (ed) New York City, NY

Ash TG (1994) In Europe's name: Germany and the divided continent. Vintage Publishers, New York

Redburn T (1993) Germany blazes an industrial trail east. The New York Times, The New York Times Company, New York 5 March 1993

Jehl D (1994) Conflict in the balkans; Clinton outlines U.S. interest in Bosnia air strikes. The New York Times, The New York Times Company, New York 10 Feb 1994

Cox M (1998) The right to return home: international intervention and ethnic cleansing in Bosnia and Herzegovina. Int Comp Law Q 47:599–631. Cambridge University Press, Cambridge, UK

The Economist (1995) Enter the Americans: America's peace plan for Bosnia is gaining support. The Economist (US edition), The Economist Newspaper Ltd.London, 19 Aug 1995

Shugarman DP (2006) Chomsky's rejection of humanitarian intervention. Working paper presented at the 2006 annual meeting of the Canadian political science association, York University, Canadian Political Science Association, Ottawa, ON

UN Security Council (1998) 3930th meeting. Resolution 1199 (1998). Available: Readex/Index to United Nations Documents and Publication. (S/RES/1199). 23 September 1998

Bjorna C (2009) Legitimising the use of force in international politics: Kosovo, Iraq and the ethics of intervention. Routledge, London

Blair T (1999) Doctrine of the international community. Speech delivered in front of the Chicago economic club, April 24 1999. Retrieved October 3, 2009 from http://www.number10.gov.uk/Page1297

Clinton WJ (1999) Remarks announcing airstrikes against Serbian targets in the federal republic of Yugoslavia (Serbia and Montenegro). The public papers of the president. The United States Government Printing Office, Washington 24 Mar 1999

Domagala A (2004) Humanitarian intervention: the utopia of just war? The NATO intervention in Kosovo and the restraints of humanitarian intervention. The sussex European institute working papers. University of Sussex, Brighton, UK

Wolfgram MA (2008) Democracy and propaganda: NATO's war in Kosovo. Eur J Commun 23(2):153. Sage Publications, London

Bellamy AJ (2002) Kosovo and international society. Palgrave, Basingstoke

Scharf MP (1999) The indictment of Slobodan Milosevic. The American Society of International Law, Electronic Publications, June 1999. Retrieved online, April 22nd 2010 from http://www.asil.org/insigh35.cfm. The American Society of International Law, Washington, DC

Krauthammer C (1985) When to intervene: what's worth fighting for? The New Republic, 192, CanWest Global Communications, Winnipeg, CA pp. 10–13

Schlafley P (1999) Clinton's post-impeachment push for power: how Clinton is using Kosovo. Phyllis Schlafley Report 32(8). The Eagle Forum, Alton, IL p. 1

Williams AB, Delli Carpini MX (2000) Unchained reaction: the collapse of media gatekeeping and the Clinton–Lewinsky scandal. Journalism Vol. 1 (1). Sage Publications, London

Nayaran, R (2000). The east timor crisis. China Report 2000; Vol 36 Sage Publications, London p. 93

UN Security Council (1999) 4045th meeting. Resolution 1264 (1999). Available: Readex/Index to United Nations Documents and Publication. (S/RES/1264). 15 September 1999

Fernandes C (2008) The road to INTERFET: bringing the politics back In. security challenges, 4(3) (Spring 2008), Konkoda Foundation, Canberra, AU pp. 83–98

KPP HAM (2002) Report of the Indonesian commission of investigation into human rights violations. Judicial system monitoring programme. Dili, ET: JSMP. Retrieved January 19th 2010 from http://www.jsmp.minihub.org/Resources/2000/KPP%20Ham%20(e).htm (Ch. II p. 6ff.)

Wheeler NJ, Dunne T (2001) East timor and the new humanitarian interventionism. Int Aff (Royal Institute of International Affairs 1944-), 77(4), (Oct. 2001) Blackwell Publishing, London pp. 805–827

Howard J (1999) Howard addresses Australian nation. Sunday, September 19, 1999. Full Transcript retrieved from *BBC News Online* http://usproxy.bbc.com/2/hi/asia–pacific/451564.stm. London: British Broadcasting Cooperation

McDougall D (2002) Australia's peacekeeping role in the post-cold war era. Contemporary Southeast Asia, December 2002. Institute of Southeast Asian Studies, Singapore

Ahmed NF (2006) UN humanitarian intervention in east timor. A critical appraisal. entelequia, revista interdisciplinar, No. 2 Fall Malaga. ES: Eumed

McLachlan I (1997) Australia's strategic policy 1997. Office for the minister of defense. Parliament House, Canberra, AU

Dept. of Foreign Affairs and Trade. (1997). In the National Interest: Australia's foreign and trade policy : White Paper. Canberra: Commonwealth of Australia

Vesel D (2004) The lonely pragmatist: humanitarian intervention in an imperfect world. Brigham Young University J Public Law, vol 18 (1 Provo, UT: BYU Law), pp. 1–58

Woods JL, Reese TR (2008) Military interventions in sierra leone: lessons from a failed state. The long war series occasional paper 28. Combat Studies Institute Press US Army Combined Arms Center, Fort Leavenworth, KS

UN Security Council (2000) 4099th meeting. Resolution 1289 (2000). Available: Readex/Index to United Nations Documents and Publication. (S/RES/1289). 7 February 2000

Ploughshares (2002) Sierra Leone (1991—first combat deaths). Armed conflicts report. Last updated 2002. Retrieved January 20th, 2010 from http://www.ploughshares.ca/libraries/ACRText/ACR-SierraLeone.html. Ploughshares Project, Waterloo, ON

Bellamy AJ, Williams PD (2005) Who's keeping the peace? International security, 29(4) (Spring 2005), Belfer Center for Science and International Affairs, Cambridge, MA, pp. 157–195

Blair T (2000) Britain's role in Sierra Leone. Press statement of the prime minister, broadcasted May 19, 2000. Retrieved January 20th, 2010 from http://news.iciba.com/patch/listen/listen_arc.php?aid=6582

Shah A (2001) Sierra Leone. Global issues. Last updated 23 July 2001. Retrieved online October 10th, 2009 from http://www.globalissues.org/article/88/sierra-leone

Kampfner J (2003) Blair's war. The Free Press, London

Evoe PJ (2008) Operation palliser: the british military intervention into Sierra Leone, a case of a successful use of western military interdiction in a sub-sahara African civil war. MA graduate thesis. Texas State University, San Marcos, TX

Pilger J (2000) Our soldiers aren't in Sierra Leone for the sake of morals or democracy. They are there for the control of diamonds. New Statesman, 29 May 2000. Spencer Neal, London

Coates D, Krieger J (2004) Blair's war. Polity Press, Cambridge

Roberson WG (2007) British military intervention in Sierra Leone: a case study. MA graduate thesis. Combat Studies Institute Press US Army Combined Arms Center, Fort Leavenworth, KS

UN Security Council (2001) 4370th meeting. Resolution 1368(2001). Available: Readex/Index to United Nations Documents and Publication. (S/RES/1368). 12 September 2001

Chesterman S (2003) Humanitarian intervention and Afghanistan. In: Welsh JM (ed) Humanitarian intervention and international relations. Oxford University Press, Oxford

Wheeler N (2004) Humanitarian intervention after 9/11. In: Lang Anthony (ed) Humanitarian intervention. Georgetown University Press, Georgetown

McInnes C (2003) A different kind of war? September 11 and the united states' Afghan war. Rev Int Stud, 29(2) (Apr. 2003), Cambridge University Press, Cambridge, UK, pp. 165–184

Bush GW (2001) Address to the nation announcing strikes against Al Qaida training camps and taliban military installations in Afghanistan. (7 October 2001). The American Presidency Project, Washington Retrieved online, October 26th 2009 from http://www.presidency.ucsb.edu/ws/index.php?pid=65088#

AEI(2008) America and the war on terrorism. AEI studies in public opinion, updated 24 July, 2008. American Enterprise Institute for Public Policy Research, Washington

UN Security Council (2002). 4644th meeting. Resolution 1441(2002). Available: Readex/Index to United Nations Documents and Publication. (S/RES/1441). 8 November 2002

Roth K (2004) War in Iraq: not a humanitarian intervention. HRW world report, Jan 2004. Human Rights Watch, NewYork, NY

Bush GW (2003) Address to the nation on Iraq. (17 March 2003). The American Presidency Project, Washington Retrieved online, October 26th 2009 from http://www.presidency.ucsb.edu/ws/index.php?pid=63713&st=&st1

Ravi N (2005) Looking beyond flawed journalism: how national interests, patriotism, and cultural values shaped the coverage of the Iraq war. Harvard Int J Press/Politics 2005, 10Sage Publications, London, p. 45

Norris P et al. (2003) Framing terrorism. Routledge, New York, Ch. 14

Mednicoff DM (2006) Humane wars? international law, just war theory and contemporary armed humanitarian intervention. Law, Culture and the Humanities 2 Sage Publications, London, p. 373 ff

Acharya A (2003) The war in Iraq: morality or the national interest? IDSS commentaries, (11/2003). The Institute of Defense and Strategic Studies, Singapore

Barnett M (1997) The UN security council, indifference, and genocide in Rwanda. Cultural anthropology, 12(4) (Nov. 1997), Wiley, Hoboken, NJ, pp. 551–578

Clinton WJ (1994) Remarks on the situation in Rwanda, 30 April 1994. The American presidency project. Retrieved online October 29th, 2009 from http://www.presidency.ucsb.edu/ws/index.php?pid=50079&st=Rwanda&st1

Mackintosh A (1996) The international response to conflict and genocide: In: David Millwood Lessons from the Rwanda experience . J Refugee Stud 9(3) Oxford University Press, Oxford, pp. 334–342

Hilsum L (1996) Reporting Rwanda—the media and the aid agencies. Paper prepared for the joint evaluation of emergency assistance to Rwanda, study III (1996, vol 3). The steering committee of the joint evaluation of emergency assistance to RwanÚ

Shibata MY (2006) A case study on the US policy in humanitarian intervention: Somalia, Rwanda, and Liberia. A research report (AU/ACSC/616-7978/AY06). USAF Air University, Maxwell, AL

Wrage SD (2000) Genocide in Rwanda: draft case study for teaching ethics and international affairs. CIAO Columbia Int Aff Online. Available online at www.ciaonet.org/isa/wrs01/ (Retrieved November 1st, 2009). Columbia University Press

Hagan J, Rymond-Richmond W (2009) Darfur and the crime of genocide. Cambridge University Press, Cambridge, MA

Prunier G (2007) Darfur—the ambiguous genocide. Cornell University Press, Ithaca

Daly MW (2007) Darfur's sorrow—a history of destruction and genocide. Cambridge University Press, Cambridge MA

UN Security Council (2004) 5015th meeting. Resolution 1556(2004). Available: Readex/Index to United Nations Documents and Publication. (S/RES/1556). 30 July 2004

UNAMID (2009) African union—united nations mission in Darfur [Official Homepage] Darfur-UNAMID- facts and figures. Retrieved July 1st 2009 from http://www.un.org/Depts/dpko/missions/unamid/facts.html

Straus S(2005) Darfur and the genocide debate. Foreign Aff, 84(1), Council on Foreign Relations, Washington, pp. 123–133

HRW (2005) Human rights watch world report 2005. Human Rights Watch, New York

US Department of State (2004) Powell reports sudan responsible for genocide in Darfur. Distributed by the bureau of international information programs, U.S. Department of State. Web site: http://usinfo.state.gov. Retrieved June 26th 2009 from http://www.america.gov/st/washfileenglish/2004/September/20040909115958JTgnilwoD0.5094873.html

Williams PD, Bellamy AJ (2005) The responsibility to protect and the crisis in Darfur. Security Dialogue, Int Peace Res Inst, 36 Sage Publications, Oslo and Washington

Grono N (2006) Briefing—Darfur: the international community's failure to protect. African Aff 105/421, Oxford University Press, Oxford, pp. 621–631

PIPA (2005) The Darfur crisis: African and American public opinion. (June 29, 2005). Program on international policy attitudes (PIPA) and Globescan report. Knowledge Networks, Menlo Park, CA

Martin R (2002) Sudan's perfect war. Foreign Aff 81(2) (Mar.–Apr. 2002), Council on Foreign Relations, New York, pp. 111–127

Blunt E (2004) What drives US policy in Sudan? BBC news, 30 June 2004. Retrieved January 29, 2010 from http://news.bbc.co.uk/2/hi/africa/3853671.stm

Chapter 4
Quantitative Analysis

As the Chap. 3 has given a detailed analysis of each individual case of humanitarian intervention, this chapter will evaluate these results in a cross-case analysis. Quantifying the qualitative findings of the previous chapter, it will be possible to make more general statements about what triggers Western democracies to intervene or abstain from intervention in humanitarian crisis.

4.1 General Findings

By defining a uniform set of parameters that is applied to each case and assigns values to each of the parameters I am able to conduct systematic comparisons both within the cases of intervention/non-interventions as well as between the intervention and non-intervention cases, thus providing a more comprehensive view on the phenomenon of humanitarian intervention. In addition to the real values, the calculated ratio between altruism and national interest clarifies to what extent either altruism or national interests played a greater role in the overall motivation for intervention.

Looking at the total numbers presented in Table 4.1, Operation *Iraqi Freedom* (Iraq) presents the highest degree of national interests and in the same time the lowest degree of altruism in comparison to other cases of intervention. Operation *Restore Hope* (Somalia) on the contrary presents the highest degree of altruism involved in the motivation to intervene. The hypothetical US intervention in Rwanda shows the lowest degree of national interests of all cases presented in this book. From the actual interventions Operation *Allied Force* (Kosovo), Operation *Restore Hope* (Somalia) and Operation *Provide Comfort* (Northern Iraq) show the lowest degree of national interests.

Looking at the numbers in relative terms presented in Fig. 4.1, however, one can make a more robust statement about the significance of the various values for the particular cases. Both Operation *Iraqi Freedom* (Iraq) and Operation *Enduring Freedom* (Afghanistan) stick out as they present the ratios that show the strongest

A. Krieg, *Motivations for Humanitarian Intervention*, SpringerBriefs in Ethics,
DOI: 10.1007/978-94-007-5374-7_4,

Table 4.1 Case Overview

	Public awareness and media coverage	Existence of an acute humanitarian crisis	Feeling of moral obligation to intervene by the decision-maker	Total amount altruism	Economic interest	Geo-strategic interest	Political interest of the decision maker	Total amount national interest	Ratio of NI & altruism in %
Northern Iraq	3,5	2,5	1	7	0	4	1	5	58:42
Somalia	2,5	4,5	4	11	1,5	0	4	5,5	67:33
Haiti	2	3	0	5	3	3	3	9	36:64
Rwanda (FR)	0,5	3	0	3,5	0	5	2,5	7,5	32:68
Bosnia	3	4	0	7	1,5	4	2,5	8	47:53
Kosovo	1,5	3	0	4,5	0	4,5	1	5,5	45:55
East Timor	4,5	4	0	8,5	2,5	3,5	1	7	55:45
Sierra Leone	1	2,5	2	5,5	1,5	4	2	7,5	42:58
Afghanistan	0	1,5	0	1,5	0	4,5	2	6,5	19:81
Iraq	0	1	0	1	4	5	2,5	11,5	08:92
Rwanda (US)	0	4	0	4	0	0,5	0	0,5	89:11
Darfur	2,5	5	0	7,5	1,5	0	0,5	2	79:21

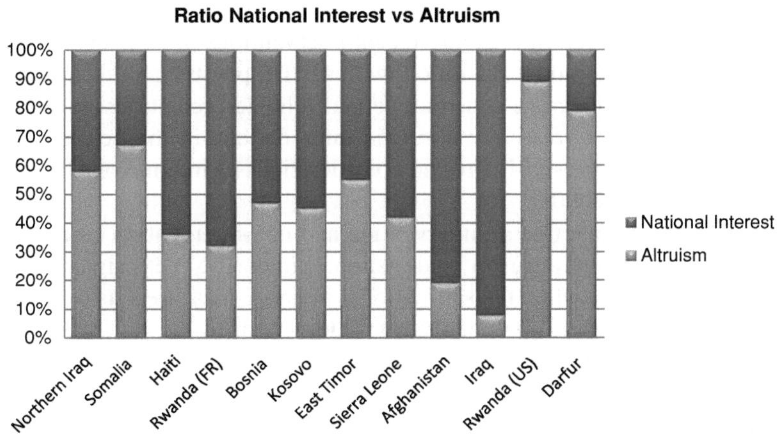

Fig. 4.1 Ratio National Interests vs Altruism

tendency towards national interests. In case of Operation *Iraqi Freedom* (Iraq) the ratio (08:92) shows that the motivation to intervene was comprised by 92 % of national interest considerations and only by 8 % of altruistic considerations.[1] The ratio in case of Operation *Enduring Freedom* (Afghanistan) (19:81) shows a similar strong tendency towards national interests, making the humanitarian character of the intervention doubtful, as well.

The two non-intervention cases analyzed in this book (highlighted in Table 4.1.), demonstrate the exact opposite from the interventions in Afghanistan and Iraq, since all four cases present ratios that have an obvious tendency towards altruism. In particular the motivation of the United States to intervene hypothetically in Rwanda in 1994 would have consisted by 89 % of altruistic considerations; and only by 11 % of national interest considerations.

In the other intervention cases analyzed in this study the ratio is more or less equally comprised of altruism or national/self-interests, while most ratios suggest that overall the tendency towards national/self-interests is dominant.

When displayed graphically in a bar chart, as in Fig. 4.1, the dominance of national interests in relation to altruism in the motivation to intervene in humanitarian crisis becomes obvious. Bearing in mind that the cases of Rwanda (US) and Darfur constitute non-intervention cases, the fraction of altruism in the motivations driving actual interventions is small. Looking at the ratio over time, one can identify a trend that suggests that altruism, though being strong in the first two interventions in Northern Iraq and Somalia, has been continuously on the

[1] These observations only hold in case all parameters are weighted equally. Results might become even more extreme, i.e. might tend more towards the national interests side, if one decides to weight the parameters differently.

retreat since the devastating 'Blackhawk Down' experience during Operation *Restore Hope* in Somalia. In the more recent interventions in Afghanistan and Iraq the degree of altruism finds its historic low mark. Despite the fact that the number of cases is too small to make constructive and reliable predictions, it seems as if the initial euphoria for relatively altruistic interventions in the beginning 1990s had to give way to more self-interested considerations in international relations in the beginning of the 2000s.

Overall, one can state that all intervention and non-intervention cases present a certain degree of both altruism and national interests. Yet, significantly, no intervention took place when the self/national interests measure was overall below the value of 2. Moreover, none of the non-intervention cases presented any geo-strategic or economic interests that were significantly strong to make the overall national interest measure surpass the threshold of 2. In addition, interests of political decision makers in these non-intervention cases were either absent or even obstructed intervention. Similarly, all non-intervention cases lack feelings of moral obligation to intervene on the side of the decision maker. Hence, one can assume that the stand point of the political decision maker in the potential intervening state towards the humanitarian crisis and his emotional involvement in the humanitarian crisis is a crucial factor in the decision making process. Intervention becomes more likely if the decision maker perceives that intervention serves his political interest and/or is personally touched by the grievances of the endangered population.

The analysis also provides interesting information in terms of internal case comparisons. Most cases were characterized by high scores on the parameter expressing the urgency of the humanitarian crisis and the way the humanitarian crises was addressed as well as on the parameter displaying the existence of geo-strategic interests. Thus, especially the actual intervention cases were predominantly motivated by the existence of an actual humanitarian crisis on the altruism side and by geo-strategic interests on the national interests side.

Displaying the data of Table 4.1 graphically, the results become even more demonstrative and concrete. In Fig. 4.2 the data is presented in a two-dimensional coordinate system that allows showing both the values on the altruism side and values on the national interest side. The results of the qualitative research can now be easily displayed and compared to each other.

At first glance, one can identify, based on the scatter plots, three different groups that are located differently in the coordinate system. Group 1 can be identified by the green data points, group 2 has blue data points and group 3 has red data points. Group 1 is comprised of the non-interventions in Rwanda and Darfur. Group 2 is comprised of the intervention in Somalia, East Timor, Northern Iraq, Bosnia, Sierra Leone, Haiti, Kosovo and Rwanda. Group 3 is made up by the inventions in Afghanistan and Iraq. Group 2 can be identified as the main group as its data points are scattered around the equilibrium. Group 1 and group 3 have to

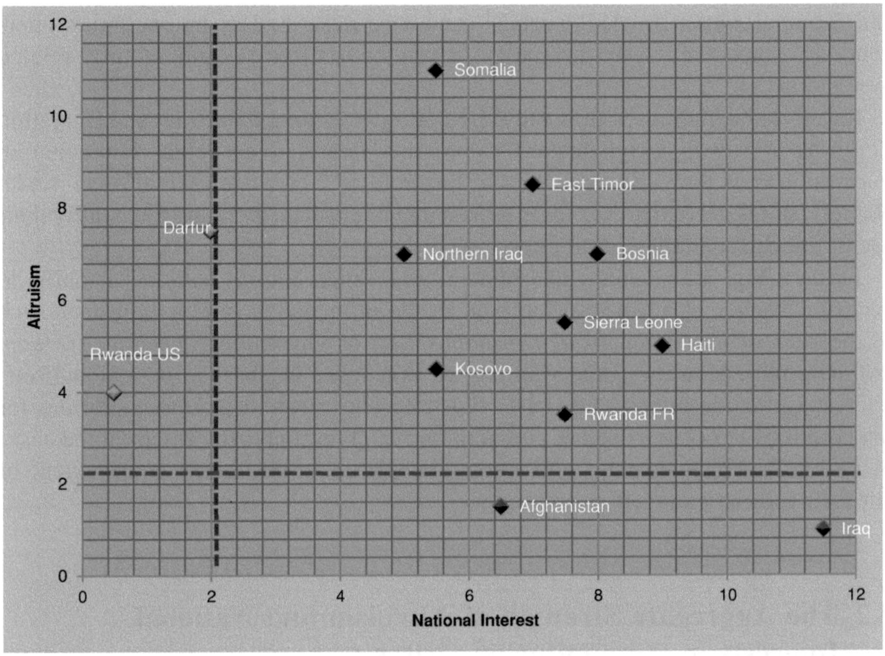

Fig. 4.2 Graphical presentation of Table 4.1

be considered as deviant cases that deviate strongly from the equilibrium. The data points of group 1 show a stronger tendency towards the y-axis (altruism) while the data points of group 3 show a stronger tendency towards the x-axis (national interests). Looking at the characteristics of the cases in group 1 and group 3, one discovers that group 1 and group 3 are comprised of the non-intervention cases and the predominant national-interest driven interventions respectively.

The first conclusion one can derive from this observation is that potential intervening states refused to intervene in cases that could not present a higher degree of national interest than 2 overall. That is to say, in order for states to consider the option of intervening in a humanitarian crisis, it is not sufficient that humanitarian crises present a set of altruistic motivating factors. States apparently require a minimum degree of national interests present to consider intervention. The reason appears to be that these interests-related motivating factors help legitimizing the substantial costs attached to intervention *vis-à-vis* the public. All intervention cases show an overall degree of national interests that is above the value of 4, 5. Thus, the non-intervention cases were lacking 2, 5 points on the national interests scale in order to qualify for military intervention.

In regards to group 3 another conclusion can be made: consistent with positions presented in the humanitarian intervention literature, both the intervention in Iraq[2]

[2] Roth (2004) Op. Cit. 405 (p. 6).

and the intervention in Afghanistan[3] cannot be described as humanitarian interventions, since they were primarily driven by retributive and security-related motivations.

Based on the findings in this study, Operation *Iraqi Freedom* (Iraq) and Operation *Enduring Freedom* (Afghanistan) cannot be identified as actual humanitarian interventions as they do not surpass a threshold of 2 points on the altruism scale. Namely, states need to present a certain degree of altruism (>2) so as to qualify their use of force as a humanitarian intervention.

Further, Fig. 4.2 suggests that humanitarian interventions can and actually do occur in absence of altruism or only under the influence of minimal altruism such in the case of Operation *Iraqi Freedom* (Iraq) or Operation *Enduring Freedom* (Afghanistan). However, interventions do not occur in absence of national/self-interest as the non-intervention cases illustrate. The most auspicious conditions for interventions to occur as actual humanitarian interventions are present in the cases of Group 2, which display motivations comprised to an almost equal extent of altruism and national/self-interests.

4.2 The Aggregate Strength of Altruism and National Interests in Humanitarian Crises

To facilitate the understanding of the aggregate motivation of the presented intervention and non-intervention cases one has to combine both the altruism and national-interest values. In this book the altruism values will be deducted from the national interest values in order to obtain the value describing the overall motivation of the particular case. The results can be found in Table 4.2 and are displayed in Fig. 4.3. Every case that scores a value above 0 was motivated by an aggregate motivation based on national interests while every case scoring below the value of 0 can be defined as an overall altruistic intervention.

In terms of national interests both the intervention in Afghanistan and Iraq show the highest scores, whereby Operation *Iraqi Freedom* (Iraq) in particular takes a very extreme position on the scale. Both Operation *Restore Hope* (Somalia) and the non-intervention case of Darfur constitute the most extreme cases on the opposite side of the scale, i.e. present overall the most altruistic motivation. It is also worth noting that all non-intervention cases are located on the altruism side, stating that all these intervention if taken place would have been overall altruistic. Apart from Operation *Restore Hope* (Somalia), Operation *Provide Comfort* (Northern Iraq) and Operation *Stabilise* (East Timor) all interventions have been motivated predominantly by national interests. Nonetheless, one can surprisingly remark that against realist belief, altruism does play a role in international relations

[3] Chesterman (2003a), (b). Op. Cit. 390 (p. 170).

Table 4.2 Overview over the aggregate strength of Altruism and National Interests in the 15 cases

	Northern Iraq	Somalia	Haiti	Rwanda FR	Bosnia	Kosovo	East timor	Sierra leone	Afghanistan	Iraq	Rwanda US	Darfur
Overall national interest	5	5,5	9	7,5	8	5,5	7	7,5	6,5	11,5	0,5	2
Overall altruism	−7	−11	−5	−3,5	−7	−4,5	−8,5	−5,5	−1,5	−1	−4	−7,5
Aggregate strength	−2	−5,5	4	4	1	1	−1,5	2	5	10,5	−3,5	−5,5

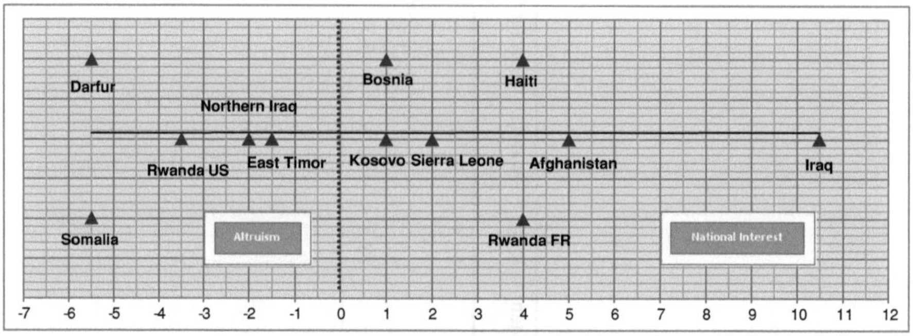

Fig. 4.3 Graphical presentation of the aggregate strength of Altruism and National Interests

	All cases	Only intervention cases
Mean	0,79	1,85
Median	1	1

and even serves as the prime motivator for three military interventions in the 1990s (Table 4.2).

Looking at the mean and the median[4] of the humanitarian intervention cases one can come to an even more pregnant conclusion about the general nature of humanitarian interventions since the end of the Cold War.

Even including the highly altruistic non-intervention cases, the overall mean of all cases is 0,79 and thereby above 0, indicating that on average all cases analyzed in this book have a slight tendency to be national interests based. The median suggests that all cases have been around the value of 1, indicating that most humanitarian interventions in the last two decades show a slight tendency towards national/self-interest. Focusing on the actual intervention cases, only, the picture becomes clearer and the results become more realistic. A mean of 1, 85 clearly signifies that all actual humanitarian interventions have had a tendency to be national interest based and not primarily motivated by altruism. Also the median of 1 indicates that national self-interest took precedence over altruism in the states' considerations to intervene for humanitarian purposes.

4.3 Discussion

The results presented above reveal the discrepancy between the normative debate discussing how the motivation for a just intervention ought to be and the empirical findings showing what actually motivated and drove humanitarian interventions in

[4] The mean and median were calculated based on the data presented in Table 4.2.

the post 1990-era. The analysis presented in this book, based on findings derived from all actual and potential humanitarian interventions between 1991 and 2010, leads to the conclusion that altruism as well as national/self-interest play a role in the motivation to intervene. Against the belief expressed by most realists that altruism does not exist in international relations, altruism has been either partially or predominantly driven states in the post-Cold War era to intervene in humanitarian crises. That is to say, other-oriented behaviour, in these cases the moral obligation to help individuals in need, is an important factor not only on the interpersonal level but also on the interstate level. Nonetheless, pure altruism cannot be observed in any of the cases presented in this study and appears therefore to be rather idealistic. Ultimately, self-interests or national interests are decisive dynamics in international relations, also in the decisions to intervene to help people in need. In this book I even showed that, unlike altruism, national/self-interests can exist on their own as a sole motivation for intervention as in the cases of Iraq and Afghanistan, where the level of altruism was not noteworthy.

In favour of the tenets of realism this book affirms that states always require a certain degree of national/self-interests so as to make a positive decision towards intervention. Due to the fact that humanitarian interventions do entail substantial costs, both financially and in terms of lives, governments have to justify their risk-taking and the investment of the nation's assets in front of the public by presenting a specific benefit.[5] Hence, the purest form of altruism as promoted and advocated by Christian scholars, organizations or institutions, who foresee a form of altruism that involves putting harm on oneself for the benefit of others, appears to remain in the realm of normative theory. Governments, despite being concerned about the distress of non-citizens outside the realm of their own nation state, would not want to inflict harm on the taxpayer or the serving soldier solely for the benefit of others.

Notwithstanding the fact that national self-interests play a crucial role in international relations, I tried to demonstrate that overall altruistic interventions do exist, i.e. there are interventions that present a higher degree of altruism than national interests. The three cases of Operation *Restore Hope* (Somalia), Operation *Provide Comfort* (Northern Iraq) and Operation *Stabilise* (East Timor) come the closest to the liberal ideal of humanitarian intervention motivated predominantly by the urge to assist people in need. In fact, the US intervention in Somalia 1992 appears to be the most altruistic case overall, showing that even an overwhelming high degree of altruism can trigger intervention. The two interventions in Northern Iraq and in Somalia were the first humanitarian interventions of its kind in the post-Cold War era and came about at a time when the United States as the only remaining superpower was trying to redefine its role in the international arena. Thus, the interventions in Northern Iraq and in Somalia stand out as they occurred at a time when peace, stability and humanitarianism took precedence over the mere pursuance of national interests. The shocking experience of the 'Black Hawk Down Incident' in Somalia and the realization that the concept of humanitarian

[5] Boettcher (2004) Op. Cit. 171 (p. 333).

intervention falls short of being an idealist bloodless war might have changed the US American perspective in a way that national interests became a major cornerstone of foreign policy again. The release of PDD 25 and the following US National Security Strategies seemed to have emphasized the importance of national interests for US foreign policy and therefore might have made predominantly altruistic interventions impossible.[6] All intervention cases following Operation *Restore Hope* (Somalia) 1992 have been overall more national interests oriented. Australia's intervention in East Timor 1999 is the last intervention case that presents an overall altruistic motivation.

Even though all interventions taken together are on average more self-interested than altruistic, the relative high degree of altruism involved in all interventions, apart from those in Afghanistan and Iraq, qualifies all other interventions analyzed in this book as just from a cosmopolitan point of view The presence of a valid *casus belli* and an other-oriented motivation makes all interventions, apart from those in Afghanistan and Iraq, at least in moral terms legitimate. Due to the vagueness of international law and the vagueness of its formulation of the concept of humanitarian intervention, it remains difficult to define the legal legitimacy of these interventions. Nevertheless, all interventions that can be found in Group 2 of Fig. 4.2 present a strong case for the use of force based on their humanitarian character.

References

Boettcher WA (2004) Military intervention decisions regarding humanitarian crises: framing induced risk behaviour. J Conflict Resolut 48:331. Sage Publications, London

Chesterman S (2003a) Just war or just peace?: humanitarian intervention and international law. Oxford University Press, Oxford

Chesterman S (2003b) Humanitarian intervention and Afghanistan. In: Welsh Jennifer M (ed) Humanitarian intervention and international relations. Oxford University Press, Oxford

Roth K (2004) War in Iraq: not a humanitarian intervention. HRW world report. Human Rights Watch, NY

The White House (1994) Presidential decision directive (PDD) 25. Clinton administration policy on reforming multilateral peace operations. US Department of State, Washington

[6] The White House (1994).

Chapter 5
Conclusion

Against the background of the disintegration of the Eastern Bloc, the disappearance of the 'Communist peril' and early traces of globalization, the leaders of the United Nations and the Western powers were seeking a new approach to international relations in an international arena that was believed to have the potential to become more peaceful and more stable. When US President Bush declared in 1990 that the world was entering a new era under a new world order, particularly the Western world was confident that in the time to come international relations would be dominated by global unity, common assistance, international justice and international peace. Within this mindset, the United States enabled the occurrence of a new phenomenon in international relations: military humanitarian intervention. Instead of merely deploying military forces abroad to defend vital national interests or to consolidate influence in a strategically important region, the US intervened in Northern Iraq in 1991 for the first time to save the lives of endangered individuals.

As humanitarian intervention has occurred in an era where international law was predominately concerned with the protection of the rights of states and did only little to defend the rights of individuals, the concept of humanitarian intervention appeared in a grey area of international law. Despite various attempts to reform international law such as Boutros Ghali's Agenda for Peace or the Responsibility to Protect, and to make the protection of human rights an obligatory duty for all UN Member States, humanitarian intervention remains a legal exception in an otherwise statist international law. Nonetheless, humanitarian intervention has evolved throughout the last two decades into a practised and applied custom in international law. While humanitarian interventions remain legally in a grey-area, just war theory has tried to regulate interventions for humanitarian purposes by setting up moral and ethical guidelines for a righteous intervention.

Dating back to the early Middle Ages and the teachings of Augustine and Thomas Aquinas, just war theory has tried to define righteous interventions on basis of several different criteria. Predominantly, the righteousness of war

A. Krieg, *Motivations for Humanitarian Intervention*, SpringerBriefs in Ethics,
DOI: 10.1007/978-94-007-5374-7_5,

depended on the intention behind using force. Seeking peace, advancing the common good, or defending good against evil were regarded as righteous intentions to wage war. The question regarding a just cause, a righteous intention or a just motivation for intervention was approached from various angles in just war philosophy. In regards to interventions for humanitarian purposes, the righteousness of the motivation of the intervener becomes a critical criterion in just war theory. Therefore, in this book I attempted to shed light on the role of the motivation behind humanitarian intervention. It has been demonstrated that the opinion of what constitutes a righteous motivation to intervene is torn between two opposing normative theories: realism on the one hand and cosmopolitan, liberal theories on the other.

In realism the protection or maximization of national interests is considered to be the most important motivation for states to act in the international arena. From a conservative realist point of view, a state should only invest as many assets into an international crisis as the crisis renders material benefits to the intervening state. Altruistic concepts of charity or benevolence are almost entirely disregarded by realist theories as they are not believed to be valid considerations in a state's decision making process. Some realists even try to make the case that governments are ethically and morally indifferent to the suffering of individuals abroad and that therefore, intervention never occurs for altruistic or moral reasons. Applying a realist definition of national interests to the liberal theories of the social-contract, allows supporters of the discretionary association theory to follow the same reasoning. Based on Locke's notion of the social contract, the government is understood to be a mere servant of the nation. Therefore, realists argue that the government can only invest the nation's assets if the common good of the nation is served, i.e. if the intervention renders material benefits. An intervention whose costs have to be borne by the nation, however, only serve the interests of strangers, e.g. endangered populations, is not considered to be just.

In cosmopolitan theories, the interests of the state or the nation are regarded to be secondary to the interests of individuals. Based on the concept of common humanity, there should not be a distinction made between nationals and non-nationals. Due to the fact that the individual is regarded to be the most important concern in international relations, the international community should primarily advance and protect the interests of suffering individuals. Humanitarian intervention should be wholly or at least primarily guided by sentiments of a common humanity, compassion and fellow feelings. Altruism, i.e. serving the interests of individuals in need abroad, should be the prime motivation for states to conduct humanitarian interventions. Humanitarianism, concerned with delivering aid to people in need regardless of race, religion or nationality, tries to apply the criteria for the delivery of humanitarian aid to military humanitarian interventions. Impartiality and neutrality are considered to be main corner stones behind humanitarian intervention, thereby rejecting any notions of maximizing one's own interest or the interests of the nation.

Because humanitarian intervention occurred as an exception to the non-intervention principle in international law, the guidelines to this type of intervention have to be carefully defined so as to avoid abuse. Even though the normative argument about the righteous motivation and intention as the primary criteria for just intervention has been well established in the intervention literature, the literature nonetheless fails to give a cohesive answer to the empirical question of what actually motivates humanitarian intervention. In this book I have tried to give an answer to the question of what actually motivates humanitarian intervention, altruism or national/self-interest.

The results of the empirical analysis do neither fully satisfy the normative arguments raised by realism nor those made by cosmopolitanism. The empirical analysis has demonstrated that humanitarian interventions were motivated by a set of mixed motivations, comprising both altruistic and interest-related factors. Overall, however, national/self-interests have been the most powerful driving force behind the humanitarian interventions of the post-Cold War era. Nonetheless, altruism has played a significant role in motivating states to intervene as well. Against realist beliefs that altruism ought to be insignificant in international relations, in this analysis I have shown that altruism does impact the decision making process surrounding humanitarian intervention and can ultimately stimulate both individual decision makers and governments to invest both financial assets and military personnel into saving strangers. Despite the fact that governments are preoccupied with advancing the interests of own nationals and the nation at large, charity, benevolence and a sense of moral obligation can trigger altruistic interventions. In particular the US interventions in Northern Iraq (1991) and Somalia (1992) serve as a proof that regardless of the availability of national/self-interests, the suffering of individuals can trigger feelings of moral obligation to assist endangered individuals abroad. The immanence of altruism in the nature of mankind seems to incite both political decision-makers and the public to envisage the possibility of humanitarian intervention.

Despite the existence of altruism in the decision making process surrounding humanitarian intervention, national/self-interest is a constant that cannot be disregarded. Looking at the two presented non-intervention cases, it becomes obvious that altruism alone cannot justify military intervention. If intervention does neither serve the political interests of the decision maker nor economic or geo-strategic national interests, altruism cannot compensate. In cases where national/self-interests stand alone in almost complete absence of altruistic factors, intervention does nonetheless occur such as in the case of Operation *Iraqi Freedom* (Iraq) or Operation *Enduring Freedom* (Afghanistan). In compliance with realist theories, most intervention cases were predominately interest-motivated whereby altruism was merely a peripheral incentive. Therefore, cosmopolitan notions that only accept purely or predominately altruistic interventions would most likely reject most interventions of the post-Cold War era as unjust for being predominantly self-interested. Taking into account that humanitarian interventions entail real costs in terms of material and manpower, it appears to be not viable to expect governments to invest into humanitarian crises in absence of any material returns. Nevertheless, cosmopolitan theories taking a less extreme normative stance granting states the right to base their actions *inter alia* on self-interested incentives, would most likely agree that the motivation behind most humanitarian interventions presented in this book can be defined as just despite the existence of ulterior self-interested motives. Apart from the intervention cases in Afghanistan and Iraq, all interventions cases had a credible altruistic component as a motivating factor that within a mixed set of motivations contributed to the overall cosmopolitan nature of the military operation at hand.

Albeit the existence of altruistic or interest-related motivation factors, governments seem to employ a certain rhetoric depending on the circumstances in order to sell intervention to the public or the international community. In public statements addressed to the nation, decision makers have repeatedly used an interest-related rhetoric to sell the case to the public. Political decision makers seem to have the need to justify intervention *vis-à-vis* the taxpayers by the existence of national interests. In the same time, decision makers have in all cases addressed the humanitarian crisis and have tried to justify intervention in rather altruistic terms. The reference to the humanitarian crisis appears to be a crucial factor in selling the intervention to the international community. Knowing about the legal obstructions to intervene in sovereign nation-states, governments try to buy legitimacy by presenting an intervention as humanitarian. In cases of Iraq (2003) and Afghanistan, however, the humanitarian rationale was not convincing enough and did not hide the fact that these interventions were actually conventional interest-motivated military interventions. In fact, the humanitarian character of these interventions appeared as a mere side-effect of actual ulterior motives.

Hence, as humanitarian interventions have become increasingly interest-motivated over the last decade it remains the responsibility of the United Nations as the umbrella organization for the international community to reform the responsibility to protect. The duty to intervene in case of humanitarian intervention has to evolve from being an imperfect duty to become a duty that is enforceable, respected and obligatory. In order to ensure that nation states intervene in severe humanitarian crises irrespective of the presence of vital national or political interests, it must not be left to the goodwill of states to avoid or bring to hold humanitarian catastrophes. Due to the fact that altruism is only as strong in bringing about intervention as risk perception and costs are low, the potential lack of interests has to be compensated by a credible and determined humanitarian intervention regime so as to ensure in the future that humanitarian intervention occurs consistently and coherently.

MIX
Papier aus verantwortungsvollen Quellen
Paper from responsible sources
FSC® C105338

If you have any concerns about our products,
you can contact us on
ProductSafety@springernature.com

In case Publisher is established outside the EU,
the EU authorized representative is:
Springer Nature Customer Service Center GmbH
Europaplatz 3, 69115 Heidelberg, Germany

Printed by Libri Plureos GmbH
in Hamburg, Germany